HIGHLANDER

MILITARY ILLUSTRATED
HIGHLANDER
FEARLESS CELTIC WARRIORS
WRITTEN BY STUART REID

SERIES EDITOR: TIM NEWARK
COLOUR PLATES BY GRAHAM TURNER

Current titles
Marine
Stormtrooper
Rifleman
Highlander

Future titles
Ranger
SAS
Paratrooper
Commando

First published in 2000 in Great Britain
by Publishing News Ltd

UK editorial office:
Military Illustrated, 39 Store Street,
London WC1E 7DB, Great Britain

Stuart Reid has asserted his moral right
to be identified as the author of this work.

ISBN 1-903040-03-5

Designed by Glenn Howard

Printed and bound in Singapore under
the supervision of M.R.M. Graphics Ltd,
Winslow, Buckinghamshire

CONTENTS

BIRTH OF THE HIGHLANDER

About two or three o'clock in the afternoon of the 18 June 1815, a French column estimated at between 3,000 to 4,000 men advanced to the hedge which marked the forward point of the British position on the ridge at Waterloo. Waiting for them on the other side of the hedge was Sir Denis Pack's Brigade and the 92nd (Gordon) Highlanders. Until now the Highlanders had been lying down, but as the French approached they stood up, formed four deep and closed to the centre. Some witnesses initially misinterpreted this as the beginnings of a retreat, but instead the Gordons stepped forward to the hedge and poured a volley into the startled French at just 20 metres range.

More than 20 years later, one of the 92nd's officers still vividly recalled what happened next: 'The Scots Greys came up at this moment, and doubling round our flanks and through our centre where openings were made for them, both Regiments charged together, calling out "Scotland for ever," and the Scots Greys actually walked over this column, and in less than three minutes it was totally destroyed, 2,000, besides killed and wounded, of them having been made prisoners, and two of their Eagles captured. The grass field in which the enemy was formed, which was only an instant before as green and smooth as the 15 acres in Phoenix Park, was in a few minutes covered with killed and wounded, knapsacks and their contents, arms, accoutrements, &c., literally strewed all over, that to avoid stepping on either one or the other was quite impossible; in fact one could hardly believe, had he not witnessed it, that such complete destruction could have been effected in so short a time.'

The action which Lieutenant Robert Winchester had just witnessed was one of the most famous and certainly the most dramatic incident at the Battle of Waterloo and the added embellishment that some of the Gordon Highlanders actually charged into action clinging to the stirrups of the Scots Greys has passed into legend. Soldiers are traditionally sustained by invoking the example of their predecessors, whether it be a regiment's dogged defence of a position against overwhelming odds or a yet more determined attack across a bullet-swept field, and paradoxically the most powerful images are not always those of glorious victory. For most British infantry regiments, including the Royal Scots, the story of Waterloo and other battles that won the Empire, from the rocky hilltop of Gandamack to the mealie-bag barricades of Rorke's Drift, is one of grim endurance. It is a tradition of standing unflinchingly through relentless artillery fire and cavalry attacks and if necessary standing until the last cartridge has been fired and all hope is gone. The Highland regiments present at Waterloo shared fully in this particular experience and on other occasions equally stubbornly held their own ground at Maya and Balaclava, but they also boast a very distinct military tradition that is typical of the Highlander. From Quebec to the Somme, Highlanders have enjoyed a wild reputation as 'Stormers', ever ready to resort to cold steel in preference to firepower. To understand why this should be so it is necessary to go all the way back to the beginning.

SPLIT IN THE KINGDOM

The Highlands occupy about half the land mass of Scotland and traditionally the boundary between the Highlands and the Lowlands is reckoned to run along the great geological fault line slashing diagonally across the country from Dumbarton Rock on the River Clyde to Dunnottar Castle on the east coast just south of Aberdeen. Although this boundary, known as The Mounth, has been characterised as a 'stupendous and seemingly impenetrable barrier, which, like a mighty wall, stretches along the southern front of the Highlands', it is in fact nothing of the sort. It is true that there are only a few points at which an army

can be marched directly into the heart of the Highlands, such as the famous pass of Killiecrankie, but the divide is otherwise more apparent than real. The hill fringes are everywhere deeply penetrated by river valleys which provide for an easy two-way traffic by both man and beast. Moreover, beyond the Mounth, the character of the land is extremely varied and, although the central part of it is certainly made up of formidable mountain chains cut through with steep-sided glens, it also includes broad swathes of more open land forming the straths and coastal plains in the north and north-east, and on the other hand the great sea lochs and islands in the west.

While the Highland Line is popularly seen as a clearly marked frontier between the Saxon and the Gael, the actual distinction was much less dramatic. In early mediaeval Scotland, it is very doubtful whether it existed at all. The original Scots or *Scotti* were a warrior aristocracy who came from Ireland in the 4th century, established themselves in what is now Argyllshire and then in a long series of wars against the native *Caledoni*, or Picts, gradually extended their influence eastwards until Coinnach Mac Alpin was acknowledged as the High King over both peoples in AD 843 or 844.

Mac Alpin's realm did not extend south of the River Forth and it was not until the 11th century that Scotland assumed something like its present shape through the acquisition by marriage of the old British kingdom of Strathclyde and the conquest of the Saxon petty kingdom of Bernicia or Lothian. At first, the Highlands, other than the Norwegian-held Hebrides and Northern Isles, remained the heartland of this enlarged Scotland, but inevitably power slowly graduated in some measure to the more prosperous arable lands and commercial centres being established along the east coast. The country remained politically well integrated until the 14th century and it is one of the striking features of the long War of

The 92nd (Gordon) Highlanders and Scots Greys charging together at Waterloo, in an 1817 print by Captain George Jones RA, supposedly based on contemporary sketches.

Independence fought between 1296 and 1341 that there was no clear distinction made between Highlands and Lowlands.

It has been plausibly suggested that the 'small folk' whose intervention proved so effective at Bannockburn in 1314 were not a mere rabble of camp-followers, but Highland levies or *ghillies* who had initially been left in reserve because they were too poorly equipped to face the English knights. In fact, many more Highlanders were already standing in the ranks of the spearmen who bore the brunt of the battle and they had, arguably, been the mainstay of the Scots armies throughout the long war. The inability of heavy cavalry to operate in the hills meant that the larger English armies led by the three Edwards were very largely confined to the Lowlands, but many crucial battles such as Robert Bruce's victory over John of Lorne at the Pass of Brander and the decisive battle of Culblean on St. Andrew's Day 1335 were fought well within the Highland Line.

The war had begun as a power struggle between the would-be successors of Alexander III and throughout its course it retained much of the character of a civil war. While even today it is both convenient and politically expedient to depict it purely in terms of an Anglo-Scots conflict, the sad truth is that some of Bruce's most notable victories were won against other Scots armies. In the first phase of the conflict, Robert I, 'The Bruce', succeeded in uniting the country behind him at Bannockburn by the brutally simple expedient of having first defeated his domestic rivals, the Baliols and the Comyns and their surprisingly numerous supporters. When Robert I died in 1329, that fragile unity collapsed into another full-blown civil war which, with renewed English intervention, dragged on until 1341, despite Sir Andrew Moray's victory over the Earl of Atholl at Culblean.

By the end of the near 50-year conflict, the country was devastated, the old Scottish line of Mac Alpin had been replaced by a southern-based half-Norman dynasty – the Bruces and their successors the Stewarts – and worst of all, central government had been fatally weakened so that only the most tenuous control was exercised over the remoter regions such as Moray and the western Highlands.

For the first time, a 14th century chronicler drew a sour distinction between Highlanders and Lowlanders, when he characterised the former as: 'savage and untamed, rude and independent, given to rapine, ease-loving, of a docile and warm disposition, comely in person but unsightly in dress, hostile to the English people and language and even to their own nation, and exceedingly cruel, but faithful and obedient to their king and country, and easily made to submit to the law if properly governed.'

There was the rub, for proper government had all but collapsed in the Highlands. In traditional feudal fashion, the Bruces had bought and rewarded their supporters with extensive land grants and in the north and west they had been forced to treat the more powerful ones like Angus Og of the Isles as allies rather than as subjects. Naturally enough, they soon responded to the weakened government of the Bruces and later the Stewarts, by asserting more and more independence. The resultant anarchy finally came to a head in 1411 when Donald, Lord of the Isles, claimed the Earldom of Ross and was only just defeated in the hard-fought and exceptionally bloody battle of Harlaw, near Aberdeen. Thereafter, royal authority over the Highlands was once more acknowledged, if only in passing, but the damage had been done.

In 1599, King James VI employed his usual eloquence in condemning, or rather comprehensively damning the Highlands in *Basilicon Doron*, a book of advice prepared for his son and heir: 'As for the Hielands, I shortly comprehend them all in two sorts of people: the

Clansman with Lochaber Axe, based on one of a remarkable series of sketches drawn by an unknown artist in the Penicuik area during the Jacobite Rising of 1745. This one provides a particularly useful indication of the relative size of the weapon.

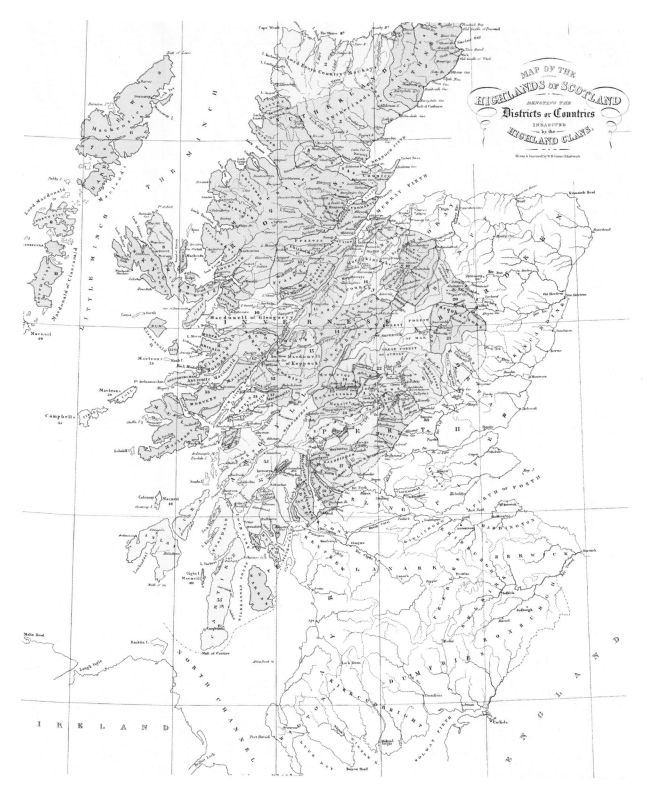

This map, produced to accompany David Stewart of Garth's *Sketches of the Highlanders of Scotland* (1822), is the most detailed and accurate depiction of both clan landholding and the 'country' associated with certain clans, not all of whom were resident on land held by their chief.

one, that dwelleth in our main land that are barbarous, and yet mixed with some show of civilitie: the other that dwelleth in the Isles and are all utterlie barbarous, without any sort or show of civilitie. For the first sort, put straitly in execution the laws made already by me against their overlords and the chiefs of their clans, and it will be no difficultie to daunton them. As for the other sort, think no other of them all than of wolves and wild boars; and therefore follow forth the course that I have begun, in planting colonies among them of answerable inlands subjects, that within short time may reform and civilise the best inclined among them, rooting out or transporting the barbarous stubborn sort, and planting civilitie in their room.'

It is, of course, easy to portray this split in dramatic terms, but language aside, in reality the growing differences between Highland and Lowland culture were far from fundamental. Rather it was a matter of degree and emphasis which reflected the way in which the one society was insular and based on a pastoral economy while the other was comparatively cosmopolitan and largely based on an arable economy. Perhaps the single best indicator of this is the tartan plaid, which well into the 18th century was being worn both above and below the Highland Line. The only difference was in the manner of wearing it. Highlanders generally left their legs bare in order to follow cattle through rough and boggy ground, while Lowlanders wore breeches underneath in order to keep the cold at bay during long days behind the plough.

CHIEF OF THE NAME

What really marked out Highland from Lowland society was its division into clans. It was the 18th century Lord President, Duncan Forbes of Culloden, who provided the clearest and most succinct definition of the Highland Clan when he described it in 1746 as: 'a set of men all bearing the same surname and believing themselves to be related one to the other and to be descended from the same common stock. In each clan there are several subaltern tribes, who owe their dependence on their own immediate chief, but all agree in owing allegiance to the Supreme Chief of the Clan or Kindred and look upon it to be their duty to support him in all adventures. As those Clans or Kindreds live by themselves, and possess different Straths, Glens or districts, without any considerable mixture of Strangers, it has been for a great many years impractical (and hardly thought safe to try it) to give the Law its course amongst the Mountains.'

At the time when Forbes was writing, the clans were very largely confined to the Highlands, or at least their fringes, but once again they were very much a Scottish rather than a purely Highland institution. They also existed in the Lowlands, or at any rate those parts of the Lowlands north of the Forth which had been comprised within the original kingdom established by Mac Alpin in the 9th century. These clans included the Forbeses, the Gordons, Graemes, Ogilvies, Douglases and Hamiltons, to name but a few of the more prominent. They may have been rather less close-knit than their Highland counterparts, but their influence and landholding frequently straddled the

Scots *schiltron* at Bannockburn 1314. Many, if not most of the spearmen in this recent reconstruction, would have been Highlanders and virtually indistinguishable from those contingents raised in notionally Lowland areas north of the Forth.

line, further blurring the largely notional distinction between Highlanders and Lowlanders.

At the head of the clan stood its *ceann-cinnidh* or chief, who might or might not bear a feudal title as Lord, Earl or Marquis, in addition to his name and territorial designation. Originally his single most important function was to lead his clan in battle. Naturally, he was not always able to do this in person and if he should be too old, infirm, ill or even mentally incapable, his place would normally be taken by his eldest son, normally distinguished as 'Young Glengarry', or 'John Campbell, Younger of Mamore', as the case might be. Alternatively, if he should be too young, leadership of the clan was temporarily vested in his guardian, usually an uncle, who bore the title of 'Tutor', as in the 'Tutor of Lovat'. In theory, there was nothing to prevent a daughter from succeeding to the leadership of a clan, but in practice this was regarded as being thoroughly unsatisfactory and the heiress was normally married off to a suitable cousin (in order to keep the land in the family) as quickly as could be decently arranged.

For the most part, the clan chiefs possessed what were regarded as the clan lands by means of a charter from the Crown. A 'piece of sheepskin' was rarely regarded as adequate title and was often required to be backed up with armed force.

Highlanders more formally arrayed for battle, as depicted in a lively sketch by the Penicuik artist in 1745. All appear to be armed with broadswords, although other sketches show firelocks and bayonets pre-dominating. Note the piper on the left.

This was particularly the case where the lands comprised in the charter included territory occupied by members of other clans. In Lochaber, for example, successive Lairds of Mackintosh received charters relating to land occupied for the most part by Camerons and MacDonalds, who refused to acknowledge their authority, preferring instead to follow their own chiefs. The Laird of Mackintosh himself was in a less than happy position since he in turn held Brae Lochaber, Moy and Larg of the Crown, and Badenoch of the Gordon Earls of Huntly, while most of his kinsmen held Strathearn from the Earl of Moray. In 1662, some Macleans, who were acknowledged tenants of The Chisholm in Strathglass, appealed over his head in a legal dispute to the chief of their name Maclean of Duart. This sort of behaviour was hardly conducive to good order. Sometimes a feud might result, such as the one between Mackintosh and MacDonald of Keppoch, which culminated in the battle of Mulroy in 1688, but more commonly the tenants played piggy in the middle to competing demands from both masters, even as late as the 1790s.

The chiefs possessed considerable powers, both as landlords and as the head of their 'name', which were generally exercised paternally, but were all too often characterised by outside observers as tyrannical. 'The chief generally resided among his retainers,' wrote Stewart of Garth. 'His castle was the court where rewards were distributed, and the most enviable distinctions conferred. All disputes were settled by his decision; and the prosperity or poverty of his tenants depended on his proper or improper treatment of them. These tenants followed his standard in war, attended him in his hunting excursions, supplied his table with the produce of their farms, and assembled to reap his corn, and to prepare and bring home his fuel. They looked up to him as their adviser and their protector.'

This authority was traditional and reinforced by

the claustrophobic nature of Highland society, but it was also given some legal force through the feudal charters by which they held their land from the Crown. This accorded to them the power of 'Pit and Gallows', which allowed and, indeed, encouraged them arbitrarily to imprison or hang lawbreakers, although this were generally reserved for outsiders. When it came to members of their own clan, eviction and expulsion was generally threat enough and if a chief demanded that a man follow his banner to war, he was in no position to refuse. The alternative was to have his cattle run off and his roof burnt over his head, yet it also appears that this was distressingly common and numerous instances are documented during the '45, and, to a lesser extent, afterwards when the chiefs wanted men for the British Army.

KIN, FRIENDS, SERVANTS, ASSISTERS AND PART-TAKERS

In a society where standing was frequently measured in terms of fighting men, the next in precedence to the chief were not the remaining members of his immediate family, but the sometimes distant cousins who headed the lesser branches of the clan: 'The cadets of his family, respected in proportion to the proximity of the relation in which they stood to him, became a species of sub-chiefs, scattered over different parts of his domains, holding their lands and properties of him, with a sort of subordinate jurisdiction over a portion of his people, and were ever ready to afford him their counsel and assistance in all emergencies.'

These men still bore the same surname, but were distinguished one from another by their territorial designations, as in Grant of Sheuglie, or Milton or Corrimony. As Garth relates, they at least paid lip service to the notion that they were all followers of their chief, but in practice some of these branches were accustomed to going their own way and were to all intents and purposes

independent clans. In the west, for example, the breaking up of the old Lordship of the Isles in the 15th century meant that the MacDonalds of Sleat, Keppoch, Clanranald and Glengarry had no acknowledged overlord, although the first was at least accorded a certain precedence. Similarly, the Campbells of Argyll and Breadalbane often found themselves at variance and some of the Laird of Grant's people also had a distressing habit of going their own way.

The immediate followers of these petty chiefs, holding farms on *tacks* or leases, were similarly designated by the name of their holding but might not always share their superior's surname. While clansmen were invariably referred to as 'being of a name', this was only a convention and although the clan map accompanying this chapter more or less accurately delineates the landholding of the several clans, they were neither confined to nor in sole possession of those lands. Since *tacks* tended to be hereditary and held for some generations, the families concerned could come to be recognised as followers or septs of a particular clan even though they might not bear its surname. The MacColls, for example, were recognised to be bound to the Stewarts of Appin while the MacRaes were held to be followers of the MacKenzie, Earls of Seaforth, and traditionally provided their bodyguards, just as the MacCrimmons provided pipers for the MacLeod. Similarly, the MacBeans, McGillivrays and other small Badenoch clans were recognised to be bound to the Lairds of Mackintosh as leaders of the Clan Chattan confederation, though perhaps not so tightly as modern tartan salesmen pretend.

Despite the notional importance attached to 'names', it was also far from uncommon to find individual *tacksmen* bearing the surnames of quite different established clans. Whilst two of the MacDonald regiments raised in 1745 by Clanranald and Keppoch were very largely officered by MacDonalds, the third, Glengarry's

A contrasting view of a Highland bowman, based on one of a series of contemporary prints by Koler, depicting Scots mercenaries in Stettin in 1631. The bow appears similar in size to the one drawn by McIan. The 'butcher knife' is probably a badly drawn dirk.

Regiment, included Mackenzies, Mackays and Grants amongst its officers. In fact, the Grants of Glenmoriston in particular (who held their land directly from the Crown), and usually the Glen Urquhart septs of Sheuglie, Corrimony and Milton, all too frequently followed MacDonnell of Glengarry rather than their own acknowledged superior, the Laird of Grant. It was even possible, if a touch unusual, to find a MacDonald holding a *tack* from a Campbell. In 1636, the celebrated Alasdair MacCholla's equally infamous father, Coll Coitach, took a *tack* of the island of Colonsay from Archibald Campbell, Lord Lorne. In addition to an annual cash rental, Coll Coitach bound himself to serve Lorne faithfully in all his lawful employments and affairs in the Highlands and Islands, by both land and sea. In this particular case, Coll Coitach was forced to accept the *tack* very largely as a means of bringing him under some sort of control. It was spectacularly unsuccessful and in 1647 Lorne, by then Marquess of Argyll, had the satisfaction of having the wicked old villain hanged. The arrangement was absolutely typical in imposing an obligation on the *tacksman* for military service whenever his superior demanded it.

A useful picture of the actual composition of a clan is provided by a casualty list compiled by Stewart of Invernahyle, enumerating the Appin men killed or wounded at Culloden in 1746. The clan regiment was led there by the Tutor of Appin, Charles Stewart of Ardsheal, and, in total, nine members of his family were killed and three others wounded. Six of Stewart of Fasnacloich's family were killed or wounded, as were no less than fifteen of Invernahyle's own kin and 13 other men named Stewart, all described as 'followers of Appin', and all presumably gentlemen.

In addition, the list also referred to a further 108 'Commoners'; the regiment's rank and file. These included 18 MacColls, 13 Maclarens,

six Carmichaels, five MacIntyres and four McInnises, but none called Stewart. In other words, two out of three men belonging to a clan regiment did not share their chief's surname.

BANGING IT OUT BRAIFLIE

Whether they were all 'of a name' or not, the Highland clans are invariably characterised as a warrior society, yet not every man in that society was a warrior. Instead, like most warrior societies, they actually comprised an agricultural peasantry dominated by a warrior aristocracy—the Highland Gentleman. Armed clashes between one clan and another might be formal, almost judicial affairs at an agreed meeting place, but normally they involved few people, comparatively little bloodshed and were largely confined to a series of raids and counter-raids, aimed at running off the other party's cattle and any other moveable goods which might be encountered in the process. Should the raiders be intercepted, a violent clash might occur, but otherwise pitched battles were a rarity. A highly developed notion of honour, ambush and assassination were the preferred methods of pursuing disputes.

Cattle raids have always been the stuff of Gaelic legend and, in Stewart of Garth's words, were 'committed by those who did not regard them as dishonourable, but exercised them at all

Cearnach: violent clashes between opposing clans normally took the form of cattle raids, assassinations and ambushes, such as this one recreated by the Wallace Clan Trust, rather than large-scale pitched battles in the open.

times, as the means of weakening or punishing their enemies.' They were usually mounted by men known as *cearnach*, or 'caterans' in Lowland Scots. The term simply means soldier, and in its origin is similar to the Irish *kern*, although in reality they were much more akin to Irish *buannacht*. Drawn from no particular strata in Highland society, they tended to be a wild lot and were widely employed for intimidation, burning, murder or even occasionally for fighting. Like the Irish *buannacht*, they generally had an unsavoury reputation as swaggering bullies and their bands all too frequently included 'broken men' owing allegiance to no clan.

'In their best days,' according to Garth, 'the *cearnachs* were a select band, and were employed in all enterprises where uncommon danger was to be encountered, and more than common honour to be acquired. Latterly, however, their employments were less laudable, and consisted in levying contributions on their Lowland neighbours, or in making them pay tribute, or *Black Mail*, for protection. The sons of the *tacksmen* or second order of gentry, frequently joined these parties, and considered their exploits as good training in the manly exercises proper for a soldier.'

It was the *cearnach*, rather than the clan gentry, who probably conformed most closely to the popular stereotype of the wild clansman and they were certainly the ones who supplied mercenary soldiers to serve all over Europe before the British Army eventually cornered the market in the second half of the 18th century. Some were no doubt bred up as *cearnach* in their fathers' footsteps, but for the most part they appear to have been a pretty promiscuous mixture of landless younger sons, idlers, thoroughgoing villains and masterless men.

Disreputable though some of them might be, the *cearnach* did not in military terms at least represent the lowest strata of Highland society.

Another study of the central figure in trews from the previous illustration, identified as Duncan MacGregor of Dalnasplutrach.

This tough-looking character, obscurely identified by the Penicuick artist as 'Shiterluck Younger', is probably intended to represent the McGhie of Sherlock who appears in the Culloden prisoner lists as commander of 'the Rannochs'.

Opposite, the combination of kilt and two-handed sword in this McIan print may again be anachronistic, but it is carefully executed and accurately shows how the kilt extends from the knees to the lower ribs.

Below them came the *ghillies* or ordinary clansmen. Those captured during the '45 or in its sorry aftermath were, generally speaking, a pretty undistinguished collection of landless labourers, herdsmen and boatmen, old men and young boys. Again, like their Irish counterparts, the *kern*, they were primarily outdoor servants rather than true fighting men, but as one of Robert Louis Stevenson's characters put it, like everyone else 'when the piper plays the clan must dance', and in a general levying out they formed the rank and file of a clan regiment.

At its most basic level, a Highland foray or *creach* might be led by a single gentleman and his sons with a gang of *cearnach* to provide the muscle and a picked handful of *ghillies* who came along not to fight but to drive off any cattle who might be encountered along the way. On the other hand, should the full strength of the clan be called out on to the heather, the existing social structure translated fairly easily into a rudimentary military one. The gentlemen called out their tenants, dependants and followers, and then acted as the officers of the clan regiment, or at the very least stood in the front rank, backed up first by the *cearnach* and ultimately by a rabble of poorly armed *ghillies* who were largely there just to make up the numbers just as Lieutenant General Henry Hawley described in 1746: 'They commonly form their Front rank of what they call their best men, or True Highlanders, the number of which being allways but few when they form in Battallions they commonly form four deep, & these Highlanders form the front of the four, the rest being lowlanders and arrant scum.'

If Hawley's language might seem a touch intemperate, it should be remembered that he was writing this passage to both educate and encourage his men before marching out to face a formidable enemy. In 1603, King James VI of Scotland had also become King James I of England, and in the Great Civil War provoked and

ultimately lost by his son, the Highlanders came to the fore as never before. Until the chaotic aftermath of the 14th century War of Independence, there is no real evidence that their style of warfare differed in any appreciable degree from other Scots troops. They had stood in the *schiltrons* at Bannockburn, but thereafter they were employed, if at all, as auxiliaries, and both equipment and tactics diverged along with the rest of their culture. In the 100-year period which began with the Great Civil War and ended on Culloden Moor, Highlanders were to earn themselves a romantic reputation as the staunchest followers of the Stuart kings. This might seem paradoxical, given the dynasty's record of alternating neglect with brutal repression, but it simply reflects the fact that in reality the Highlanders were not the first or most important allies to whom the Stuarts turned—for only a minority ever marched behind their banner—but rather that they were their last remaining ones. Consequently, Highlanders took the field in these wars not as mere auxiliaries, as they had done at Flodden and Pinkie, but as the chief strength of the Stuart armies, bringing with them a style of warfare then quite unique within the British Isles.

Braemar Castle in Upper Deeside, Aberdeenshire. A typical 'L Plan' tower house belonging to the Farquharsons of Invercauld. The outer wall dates to its period as a military post in the 18th century, but most towers boasted a similar *barmekin* wall in which to shelter cattle.

Opposite, A Highland chieftain of the late 16th or early 17th century in doublet and belted plaid, though contemporary portraits show no reluctance on their part to wear breeches.

ARMING THE HIGHLANDER

The most obvious distinguishing feature of the Scottish Highlander was his unique clothing and equipment. In the popular mind, he presents an imposing figure, striding forth from the colourful plates in McIan's *Costume of the Clans*. He is almost invariably kilted, or at least swathed in the tartan splendour of a belted plaid, worn over a shirt (frequently ragged) and sometimes a simple deerskin jerkin. As to his arms, he carries a basket-hilted broadsword with a blued-steel *Andrea Ferrara* blade, a round bull-hide targe embellished with a wicked spike in the centre, a dagger or dirk of immoderate size, a brace of steel pistols, a firelock on his shoulder, and, should all of these unaccountably fail him, a small *sgian dubh* (dirk) tucked away for emergencies.

Surprisingly enough, some of the richer and more vainglorious Highland gentlemen actually matched this romantic vision—save for very properly wearing a coat and waistcoat over the shirt—but for the most part it is an extravagant caricature. The grim reality was somewhat different.

NAKED PIKES, TARTAN COATS

As to the very earliest times, we know very little of Highland dress and arms except that the ancient *Caledoni* may have entered battle naked apart from some woad, hence their Roman nickname *Picti*—the 'painted lot'. The *caveat* should be made that 'naked' is an ambiguous term which can be rather more plausibly interpreted in a military context to mean simply that they wore no armour, rather than that they were a gang of militant nudists. Although one Roman gravestone rather conventionally depicts some nude *Caledoni* (easily identified by their distinctive square shields) being trampled under the departed hero's feet, those figures representing *Caledoni* carved on their own symbol stones and on early Christian crosses are all clad in what appear to be tunics or long coats and sometimes hooded cloaks as well.

Similarly, in the medieval period, the abundant evidence of the effigies carved on West Highland grave slabs reveals that clan gentry were conventionally dressed in knee-length *akhetons* or *gambesons* (heavily padded and quilted protective linen coats which were, according to some accounts, waterproofed with tar), mail hoods and bascinet-like helmets, and they were armed with spears and broadswords. Such men were dressed and equipped to stand in the front rank of the *schiltrons* or columns of spearmen which humbled 'Proud Edward's Army' at Bannockburn, and while it is not until the early 16th century that the first written descriptions of the ordinary clansman's clothing appears, there is good reason to suppose that they were dressed in broadly similar fashion.

The tunics seen on the early symbol stones may simply be *leine*, the voluminous linen shirts frequently mentioned by 16th century sources, but it is rather likelier that they represent the long coats still being worn in the northern Highlands as late as the 17th century. In 1521, a Highland gentleman with the name of John Major (presumably a clumsy rendering of *Iain Mor* or Big John) wrote of the 'wild Scots' having no covering for the leg from the middle of the thigh to the foot, and instead wearing a *chlamyde* or gown over a saffron shirt. These simple garments were single-breasted, knee-length or longer and sometimes sleeveless. They were made either from tartan or self-coloured woollen material and fastened by means of cloth buttons and a belt around the waist. Three out of the six Highlanders in the well-known prints published by Koler in 1631 are depicted as wearing these long coats.

The coats were probably more popular with the ordinary clansmen than is generally realised, but by the 18th century the upper part of the body was clad in a much shorter hip-length jacket, and often a waistcoat underneath. One unfortunate individual, whose corpse was discovered in a peat

bog at Quintfall Hill in Caithness, was actually found to be wearing two sets of coat and breeches, one on top of the other, which shows a rather more realistic appreciation of what should be worn on the hills than modern artists who persist in depicting clansmen wearing no more than a ragged shirt and plaid. Those who could afford them wore tartan jackets of a sett which often contrasted with, rather than matched, any other garments they might be wearing, but as they were wasteful of material and required some skill in tailoring, Stewart of Garth notes that plain coloured jackets were more common, with blue and green being particularly popular.

When the *Scotti* came from Ireland, they brought with them the *truibhs* or trews. Towards the end of the 18th century, the quite nonsensical belief was fostered by romantics that Highlanders had a violent objection to being 'stuffed into breeches', but there is little evidence this was the case. It is certainly true that Highlanders from Lochaber and the Great Glen used to be quite rude about men from Caithness and Sutherland who habitually wore breeches, but Sir James Sinclair of Ulbster believed trews were the 'ancient' dress of Highlanders and in 1794 clothed his Caithness Fencible regiment accordingly.

Trews took two forms. The more familiar style was not unlike medieval hose, close-fitting full-length leggings with integral feet. Martin Martin from Skye described them in 1703: 'Many of the People wear *Trowis*, some of them very fine Woven like Stockings of those made like of Cloath; some are coloured, and others are striped; the latter as well shaped as the former, lying close to the Body from the middle downwards, and tied around with a Belt above the Haunches. There is a square piece of Cloth which hangs down before.'

There are obvious disadvantages to wearing this kind of garment in a boggy country since getting the feet wet necessitates a complete

change and, according to an observant Englishman named Edward Burt, a chief's numerous train of followers even included a '*Gilli-casflue*' (sic) whose function was to carry his master dry-shod across fords. Not surprisingly, long trews were generally confined to Highland gentlemen who wore them indoors or on horseback, although Burt does describe them being worn *under* kilts and plaids for warmth in the winter. Other, shorter trews, including those seen in the early Irish illustrations of *Scotti*, were close-fitting knee breeches, which originally left the calves and feet bare, but by the 18th century they can frequently be seen in paintings being worn with more or less matching tartan stockings.

PLAIDS IN THE HEATHER

As to the *breachan* or tartans themselves, in 1581, George Buchanan noted: 'They delight in variegated garments, especially stripes, and their favourite colours are purple and blue. Their ancestors wore plaids of many colours, and numbers still retain this custom, but the majority now in their dress prefer a dark brown, imitating nearly the leaves of the heather, that when lying upon the heath in the day, they may not be discovered by the appearance of their clothes.'

Camouflage aside, the dull colours were probably dictated in large part by the availability of dye-stuffs which may well have encouraged the development of local patterns or setts, traditional

Opposite, A good study by McIan of a Highland gentleman in belted plaid. Of particular interest are the cuff details and the V-shaped slit in the rear of the bonnet which allowed for adjustment to individual head size.

From left to right, Highland gentleman in trews. This reconstruction shows off a number of interesting features. The side openings may have given rise to Martin's reference to a piece of material hanging down in front. Note how the trews

are in effect constructed as a pair of shorts with legs attached. This allows the best use to be made of the material and ensures the necessary degree of flexibility at the knees. Note also the knee garters and the characteristic way in which they are 'hinging

aff the arse'. The third illustration shows a cavalryman's buff coat of the style stolen by MacIan of Glencoe from the Gordon Laird of Edinglassie and subsequently worn by him at the Dalcomera gathering in 1689.

to a particular area. These may in turn have come to be associated with the clans who were resident in those areas, but it is still a long way from the heraldic exactitude of the modern concept of clan tartans. Many clan tartans do in fact predate the Victorian period, but while they are based on setts worn by the various chiefs, it does not follow that all their clansmen imitated them.

In 1689, a Jacobite volunteer named James Philip of Almerieclose was present at the great clan gathering at Dalcomera and in describing the various contingents which rallied to the Jacobite leaders, he conspicuously failed to make any mention of them all wearing the same tartans,

although he did refer to the immediate followers of the various chiefs wearing plaids with, for example, a yellow or a red stripe, or a triple red stripe. In a series of early 18th century portraits by Richard Wait, depicting the Laird of Grant and several of his kinsmen, no two of them are wearing the same sett. There is, of course, ample evidence for the use of what might be termed livery tartans. Wait's paintings of the piper and champion of the Laird of Grant, show them both to be wearing near identical setts, which are quite unlike those worn by the gentlemen, but the use of these setts will have been confined to the chief's immediate household rather than worn by his clansmen at large.

Whatever the sett, tartan was seen to best advantage in the kilt and belted plaid. Its antiquity is uncertain, for the earliest references to Highland dress seemingly relate to the coat or gown, but in 1549, a French visitor noted: 'They wear no clothes except their dyed shirts and a sort of light woollen covering of several colours'. In 1578, Bishop Leslie described it as being 'long and flowing but capable of being neatly gathered up at pleasure into folds.' This multi-coloured mantle or covering is clearly what is commonly known as the belted plaid or *breachan na feal*.

Writing in 1822, Stewart of Garth provided what might be the clearest and most comprehensive description of this simple garment: 'This was a piece of tartan two yards in breadth, and four in length, which surrounded the waist in large plaits or folds, adjusted with great nicety, and confined by a belt, buckled tight around the body; while the lower part came down to the knees, the other was drawn up and adjusted to the left shoulder, leaving the right arm uncovered, and at full liberty. In wet weather, the plaid was thrown loose, and covered both shoulders and body; and when the use of both arms was required, it was fastened across the breast by a large silver bodkin, or circular brooch... These were also employed to fix the plaid

Far left, **Highland bowman after Koler (1631), wearing a knee-length tartan coat over what appear to be trews. Note that, like the other Scots mercenaries in this series of prints, he has no sword, although he may have a dirk on his left hip.**

Left, **Highlander after Heere (c.1570s). At first sight the 'shorts' look odd but are most likely just an ordinary pair of hose. Contrast the method of carrying the sword with McIan's depiction of it carried on the back—it is actually quite difficult to draw a straight-bladed sword over the shoulder**

on the left shoulder.'

Other accounts suggest that the belted plaid could comprise up to six double ells of tartan material. Elsewhere, Garth explicitly states that it was folded in half before putting it on in order to double the thickness, but while this might explain the references to double ells, it seems doubtful. Plaiding was always woven on a 27-inch (68.5cm) width, but, as Garth notes, something like two yards, or rather a full broadcloth width of 54 inches, was actually required and something approximating it could be achieved by stitching two lengths of plaiding together in order to 'double' not the length, but the width. Even then, six Scots ells (or even the four mentioned by Garth), amounting to a total length of 5.6 metres, still produces a formidable quantity of material to be disposed of. Some 17th century portraits of tartan-clad aristocrats suggest this could be done quite flamboyantly, but doubling the thickness, as Garth suggests, provides for a much warmer and more manageable garment.

Managing it properly was in fact far from easy. In the first place, the weight of the upper part usually drags the lower hem well above the knee after a very short time, and folding the pleats 'with great nicety' can be a very tedious business, especially if it has to be done on the ground rather than on a table or other raised surface. It is also wholly impractical to attempt it in wet and windy weather. Therefore, while what purists might regard as the proper method of belting a plaid would certainly have been employed by a gentleman intending to make a good appearance, it is far easier simply to throw the plaid over the shoulders like a cloak and then belt it around the waist while standing upright. The result is far from elegant but the marked resemblance to an untidy bundle of washing can be seen in many 18th century prints.

While the plaid was obviously a useful garment, in that it required no tailoring and could serve equally well as a cloak and bedding, it could be too cumbersome if heavy or energetic work was to be carried out. Some accounts even suggest that it was common to throw it off entirely before running into battle in shirt tails, though while this was certainly done in the midsummer heat at Kilsyth in 1645, it might be a hangover from earlier periods when voluminous *leine* or saffron shirts were often worn to mark out leaders.

Something lighter and more manageable was clearly required and eventually appeared in the form of the *philabeg* or kilt. In form the early kilt is simple enough and well illustrated in some of Mclan's prints. All that is required is a single length of plaiding, extending from the knees to the lower ribs and pleated as usual at the rear. The upper third of the quite large box pleats are then sewn into place, thus permitting the whole thing to be secured around the waist with pins.

The origins of this garment have been hotly debated and, despite its simplicity, the evidence suggests that it is as late as 18th century in origin. At first, it was generally believed to have been devised by an Englishman working in Lochaber, who may or may not have been called Rawlinson. This assertion was vehemently denied by a number of writers in some vituperative correspondence which surfaced in the *Scots Magazine* in 1798, but other than some very obscure references to a mysterious garment called a *fiack,* which might just conceivably be an early kilt, no reliable evidence has emerged of its use prior to the 1720s. Indeed, it is very hard to escape the impression that the argument only arose in the first place because the supposed inventor was an Englishman rather than a Scot! Be that as it may, it can at any rate be established with some certainty that the kilt was adopted by the British Army's Highland regiments, initially as a fatigue dress, during the 1750s (which would again argue for a comparatively recent origin) and only very gradually came to supplant the belted plaid in everyday use.

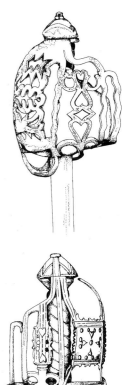

Top, typical example of a Stirling-made basket hilt for broadsword or backsword. Stirling hilts, which were generally popular in Perthshire and Badenoch, as well as in the Lowlands, were very free in style. *Bottom*, In contrast, the Glasgow or western hilt was much more formal in style and individuality was expressed in the fine detail of the pierced and incised decoration which appeared on the panels.

COLD STEEL

The fighting methods of the Highlander were by no means as straightforward as might at first appear and were once again a product of history and culture. The *Caledoni* were predominantly spearmen or rather pikemen, and there is no reason to suppose that they did not fight in *schiltrons*—a term which literally translates as moving thickets—just as their descendants were to do in the Middle Ages. Similarly, medieval West Highland effigies often depict spearmen rather than heroic swordsmen. Yet by the 17th century, a rather different fighting style had come to predominate. In the anarchy which followed the long War of Independence, the Highlands became alienated from what might be regarded as mainstream or Lowland Scots society. The clans were on their own and fell back on their old Celtic ways.

Gaelic culture centred around the warrior or individual fighting man. It is important to appreciate the differing levels of clan society. The gentlemen were quite literally heroic figures. In a large scale conflict, they would be expected to lead their men in the battle-line, but otherwise their function was to engage in formal if not ritual combat—duels—with men of similar social standing. For this, they did not require the long *schiltron* spear, but a sword and shield, or a two-handed sword, according to preference.

The earliest known Highland swords were straight-bladed weapons, distinguished by the way in which the quillons were angled towards the blade. Apparently of Norse origin, they were intended to be wielded with one hand. The term *claidheamh mor* (claymore), or big sword, served to distinguish this weapon from the original short swords variously called dirks, *dorlachs* or *sgians*, carried as a secondary weapon by *Caledoni* and *Scotti* pikemen. It should not be confused with the *claidheamh da laimh*, or great two-handed sword, which was popular for a time in the 16th and early

17th centuries. Elsewhere in Europe, the two-handed sword was a specialist weapon and there is no reason to suppose that this was not also the case in Scotland. Ultimately most of them were either cut down into broadswords or preserved as ceremonial bearing swords, though Woodhouselee claimed to have seen some carried by the clansmen who occupied Edinburgh in 1745.

The pre-eminent Highland sword remained the claymore in its ultimate form as the basket-hilted broadsword. Appearing in the mid-16th century, it did not supplant the two-handed sword but was simply a logical development of the quilloned

Opposite, Recreated clans-man with firelock. Although they were unable to engage regular troops in firefights, all Jacobite soldiers were issued with firelocks and bayonets, generally of French or Spanish origin, during the '45.

Incongruous though they might appear, this Highland gentleman and his pony are correctly depicted by McIan. Both the harness and saddle are plaited from rope, with the latter taking the form of a large oval pad covered by a goatskin.

weapon which appeared in the early Middle Ages. Normally the blade was double-edged, but single-edged backswords became quite common in the 18th century, as did a couple of quite bizarre variants. One was the *Turcael* or curved Turkish blade. Few survive, apart from those carried in the 19th century by the Light Company officers of Highland regiments, but a good example can be seen in Wait's portrait of Alasdair Mor Grant, the Laird of Grant's champion, and a surprisingly high proportion of the clansmen drawn by the Penicuik artist in 1745 carry curved blades. Another, less common variant, also illustrated in the same sketches, featured a straight blade with serrated edges, like some 16th century rapiers and *Landsknecht* swords. One of these, named 'The Brindled Wrangler', was carried by Allan Cameron of Erracht, who raised the 79th (Cameron) Highlanders in 1794, and can still be seen in the Regimental museum.

With the sword went the targe, a round shield

Regular musketeer as depicted by Jacob de Geyhn, 1607. The widespread introduction of reliable firearms in the late 16th century brought about a radical shift in Highland tactics and directly led to the development of the Highland Charge.

usually made of plywood and covered with leather. The most detailed description of one is provided in a letter written by Henry Fletcher in 1719, although it is unlikely that all were so elaborately constructed: 'The outward form of ane Highland Targe is a convex circle, about 2 foot in diameter, but some have them oval; the innermost part of it nixt the man's breast is a skin with the hair upon it, which is only a cover to a steel plate, which is not very thick, for the whole is no great weight; on the inner side of this Steel plate the Handle is fixed, which hath two parts, one that the left arm passes throw til near the elbow, the other that the Hand lays on: without the Steel plate there is a cork which covers the Steel plate exactly, but betwixt the Cork and the Steel plate there is Wooll stuffed in very hard: the Cork is covered with plain well-wrought leather, which is nailed to the cork with nails that have brass heads, in order round, drawing thicker towards the centre. From the centre sticks out a Stiletto (I know not the right name of it, but I call it so, because it is a sort of short poignard) which fixes into the steel plate and wounds the Enemy when they close: about this Stiletto closs to the Targe there is a peece of Brass in the form of a Cupelo about 3 inches over and coming halfway out on the stiletto and is fixed upon it. Within the brass there is a peece of Horn of the same forme like a cup, out of which they drink their usquebaugh, but it being pierced in the under part by the Stiletto, when they take it off to use it as a cup, they are obliged to apply the forepart of the end of their finger to the hole to stop it, so that they might drink out of their cup.'

This combination of sword and shield, or occasionally a two-handed sword, was ideally suited for individual combat, and in 1618, Grant of Ballindalloch and his men attacked a house in the burgh of Elgin (which always had something of the character of a frontier town) with what sounds like a particularly well-armed gang of *cearnach* waving a formidable collection of 'bowis, durkis, swerdis, Lochaber aixes, mailye coattis, Jedburgh staulfis, halbertis, guns, hagbutts and pistollets.' This fearsome diversity was less well adapted for more large scale warfare, when the full strength of the clan had to be pulled out on to the heather. Originally the *ghillies* may simply have been armed with pikes or *schiltron* spears, and as late as 1689, these and long-hafted axes were still the most frequently mentioned weapons in Almerieclose's description of the various western clans mustered at Dalcomera. This may also have been the case further east as well, and this is brought out in a highly revealing series of *wapinschaws*, or musters, held in Perthshire in 1638, on the eve of the Great Civil War.

Out of 451 able-bodied men in five Atholl parishes, 124—a quarter—carried both sword and targe. This more or less corresponds to the usual proportion of gentlemen and *cearnach* and their status is confirmed by the fact that 54 of them also had a musket and a bow, another 38 had muskets, and eleven just had bows in addition to their swords. As to the remaining three quarters, the fact that all but 11 reportedly had swords might at first seem vastly encouraging, but the absence of targes and the fact that they shared just five muskets and 73 bows between them, suggests that the 'swords' were in fact dirks, rather than broadswords. Nor had the situation improved a century later. An estimated 1,500 Highlanders were killed or wounded at Culloden in 1746, yet only 192 broadswords were recovered from the battlefield by clearance squads.

The starkest picture comes from an admittedly hostile account of the rebel occupation of Edinburgh by Patrick Crichton of Woodhouselee: 'I entered the town by the Bristo port, which I saw to my indignation in the keeping of these caterpillers. A boy stood with a rusty drawn sword, and two fellows with things licke guns of the

16 centurie sat on each syde the entry to the poors howse, and these were catching the vermin from ther lurking places abowt ther plaids and throwing them away. I said to Mr Jerdin, minister of Liberton, "Ar these the scownderells [who] have surprised Edinburgh by treachery?" He answered, "I had reither seen it in the hands of Frenchmen, but the divell and the deep sea are both bad."

'When I came to the head of the stairs [which] leads to the Parliament Closs I cowld scarce pass for throng, and the Parliament Closs was crowded with them, for they were to make the parad at reading the manefesto and declaration from the Cross. I saw from a window near the Cross, north syde of the High Street, this commick fars or tragic commody. All these mountain officers with ther troupes in rank and fyle marched from the Parliament Closs down to surrownd the Cross, and with there bagpipes and loosie crew they maid a large circle from the end of the Luickenbooths to half way below the Cross to the Cowrt of Gaird, and non but the officers and speciall favowrits and one lady in dress were admitted within the ranges. I observed ther armes: they were guns of diferent syses, and some of innormowows length, some with butts turned up lick a heren [i.e., like a herring] some tyed with puck threed to the stock, some withowt locks and some matchlocks, some had swords over ther showlder instead of guns, one or two had pitchforks, and some bits of sythes upon poles with a cleek, some old Lochaber axes. The pipes plaid pibrowghs when they were making ther circle. Thus they stood rownd 6 or six men deep. Perhaps there was a strategem in this appearance, to make us think they were a rabbell unarmed in this publick parad show, for a great many old men and boys were mixed, and they certainly conceiled there best men and arms thus; for they have 1400 of the most daring and best melitia in Europe.'

Both Woodhouselee's description and the

Top right, **Highland swordsman after the Penicuik artist 1745. This pugnacious-looking character in trews carries an unusually large targe and is armed with a dirk and one of the basket-hilted sabres variously referred to as *Turcael* ('Turks') or *Claidheam-crom*.**

Bottom right, **Left-handed Highlander after the Penicuik artist. Note the characteristic way in which the targe is held up to protect the head. Like most of the gentlemen, as distinct from ordinary clansmen depicted by the artist, he wears trews rather than a plaid.**

1638 *Wapinschaw* returns, summarised above, not only bear out other contemporary accounts, such as General Hawley's, which distinguish between the 'True Highlanders' or gentlemen in the front rank, and the 'arrant scum' packing in behind them, but also clearly illustrate the problem which led directly to the development of the famous Highland Charge and everything which followed from it.

THE HIGHLAND CHARGE

The problem, put very simply, was the unfortunate fact that, despite being labelled a warrior society, only about a quarter of a clan's disposable manpower was properly armed. This was of little consequence in the early medieval period when the remainder could be issued with pikes or long-hafted axes in order to take their place in the rear ranks of *schiltrons*, but as Highland society came to be alienated from the wealthier and more populous Lowlands, these levies were seldom required and the scale of Highland warfare diminished. That is not to say the area became more peaceful—if anything, the reverse was the case—but rather a switch to low-intensity warfare meant that what might be termed the professional (or at least semi-professional) fighting men, be they gentlemen or *cearnach*, came to rely upon

the weapons and fighting methods which were appropriate to it.

The process was a gradual one and there were still large-scale levies of Highland troops after Culblean. Unfortunately, we know far too little about how the battle of Harlaw was fought in 1411, but the fact that it lasted all day and that Highlanders only retired under cover of darkness, clearly points to a sustained encounter which could only have been maintained by steady pikemen rather than a volatile mob of heroic swordsmen. Nor is there any reason to suppose that the 'Highland' division commanded by Lennox and Argyle at Flodden in 1514 was not equipped with pikes, as was certainly the case with the Gordons under Huntly on the Scottish left. In December 1552, two Highland companies levied by the then Earl of Huntly for service in France were ordered to be 'substantiouslie accompturit with jack and plait, steilbonnet, sword, bucklair... and a speir of sax elne long or thairby' and at the battle of Corrichie 10 years later all of Huntly's men, both Highland and Lowland, were equipped as pikemen.

The two styles of warfare were neither exclusive nor incompatible. Amidst the prolonged slaughter of Harlaw, both sides celebrated the single-handed encounter between Sir Alexander

Opposite, The Black Watch, 1743. This reconstruction of a soldier of the 43rd Foot, better known as the Black Watch, is based on one of the well-known 'Mutineer' prints published by Bowles, depicting Corporal Malcolm MacPherson. The son of a *tacksman* in Driminard in Strathspey, MacPherson enlisted in Lord Lovat's Independent Company in 1737 and six years later he and his cousin, Samuel MacPherson, were among the ringleaders of the infamous Black Watch mutiny and were shot for it, together with Private Farquhar Shaw on 18 July 1743.

This reconstruction has been slightly altered in order to conform more closely to the detailed representation of the regimental uniform in the 1742 *Cloathing Book*, but is otherwise unchanged. MacPherson wears a typical knitted blue bonnet, red 'bob-tailed' coat, double breasted like contemporary

Dragoon coats, and a red waistcoat. The yellowish buff facings on the cuffs were worn until the regiment received its Royal designation in 1758. His belted plaid is the now familiar Black Watch or Government sett, featuring rather smaller checks than are generally seen at the present day.

The origin of this sett, which may well have given the regiment its nickname, is unknown. It was once claimed to be a Campbell sett, but early portraits showing that clan's gentlemen wearing predominantly red setts, suggest that modern Campbell tartans are derived from the Black Watch tartan rather than the other way around. The Grants and the Mackays, who were closely associated with both the early Independent Companies and those raised during the '45, also claim an interest in the sett, but the likeliest explanation is that when

General Wade ordered that the plaids of each company were 'to be as near as they can of the same sort and colour', the Captains agreed on a mutually acceptable sett and placed a bulk order with the weavers. The tartan may well have been a local pattern popular in Badenoch and Strathspey, but there is no suggestion of any clan connections.

Shortly after Lord John Murray succeeded to command of the regiment in 1745, a single red overstripe was added to the tartan, probably in order to distinguish the soldiers of the Watch from the new Highland Independent Companies raised during the Jacobite rising. Initially, the new companies (and the Argyle Militia) got by without uniforms, but eventually they were clothed very similarly to the 43rd with red jackets faced yellow, and plaids of the Government sett. Although the new com-

panies were disbanded shortly afterwards, the Black Watch retained the red overstripe until at least 1812.

The weapons displayed around the figure are typically associated with Highlanders, although only gentlemen such as MacPherson could afford to carry them in combination. The round shields called targes may well have been carried by members of the original Independent Companies, but not after they were embodied into the 43rd Foot, and while the broadsword would officially remain a part of the soldier's kit for much of the century, increasing reliance would be placed on the bayonet. Pistols were supplied at the Colonel's expense (for which he received a generous allowance from the Government), but not dirks, although their use by officers and NCOs was tolerated and even encouraged. *Painting by Graham Turner.*

Irvine of Drum and Hector Ruadh, the chief of the Macleans, and, according to a later ballad, another between Forbes of Drumminor and one of the MacDonalds. In the end, the decisive catalyst which meshed both together was the widespread introduction of firearms.

At Pinkie in September 1547, and as late as the Great Civil War in the mid-17th century, *cearnach* armed with bows served as skirmishers and provided covering fire for the gentlemen. A good example was at Auldearn in 1645, where Sir Mungo Campbell of Lawers' Regiment was 'shot' on to its objective by Mackenzie of Seaforth's bowmen standing behind it. Firearms, however, can only be used in a direct fire role and while their adoption by regular armies led to infantry tactics becoming dominated by the winning of the firefight, the Highlanders' lack of discipline and intensive training, placed them at a fatal disadvantage, as the Jacobite Adjutant General Colonel Sullivan noted: 'Any man yt ever served with the highlanders knows yt they fire but one shot & abandon their firelocks after. If there be any obstruction which hinders them of going on the enemy all is lost; they don't like to be exposed to the enemy's fire, nor can they resist it, not being trained to charge [i.e., load] as fast as regular troops, especially the English wch are the troops in the world yt fires best.'

In that single paragraph, the Irishman from County Kerry provided the starkest and clearest explanation of the rationale behind the Highland Charge. In the face of increasing firepower, there was simply no alternative but to eschew the rituals of heroic single combat and the steady advance of spearmen in favour of a headlong rush which had the dual function of carrying them over the crucial 100 metres of bullet-swept ground as quickly as possible, and at the same time, putting the fear of God into the opposition. Major General Henry Hawley, once again, provides a good description: 'When these battalions come within

a large musket shott or three score yards [say 50 metres] this front rank gives their fire, and immediately throw down their firelocks and come down in a cluster with their swords and targets, making a noise and endeavouring to pierce the body or battalion before them— becoming twelve or fourteen deep by the time they come up to the people they attack... if you give way you may give your foot for dead, for they being without a firelock or any load, no man with his arms, accoutrements &c. can escape them, and they give no Quarters.'

Hawley wrote this famous account in January 1746 in a vain attempt to prepare his men for what they were about to receive, and it is important to appreciate the extent to which the success of a Highland Charge depended on sheer intimidation rather than brute force. The popular view is that the clansmen advanced cautiously into musket range, flung themselves flat to avoid their opponents' volley and then, springing up again, charged forward to cut down the hapless soldiers while they were still struggling to reload their muskets. The image of hapless Redcoats being swept away by this 'avalanche of steel' is, however, a gross over-simplification. In reality, a close examination of the Charge's recorded successes shows that the defending troops had actually panicked and given way *before* the Highlanders reached them.

This being the case, it was perhaps of little importance whether the *ghillies* (or 'arrant scum') were well armed or not. The mixture of old and perhaps useless matchlock muskets, Lochaber axes and occasional two-handed swords described by Woodhouselee, were perfectly adequate for the purposes of intimidation and while the universal issue of French firelocks and bayonets after Prestonpans might have imparted a certain respectability to the ordinary clansmen, they did nothing to enhance their military effectiveness.

Opposite, A useful print by McIan demonstrating how the belted plaid could serve as a cloak in bad weather. In 1822, Stewart of Garth stated that Highland bonnets were much smaller than the broad 'Lowland' one as depicted here, but this is not generally borne out by Koler's prints or by archaeological finds.

HIGHLANDERS IN ACTION

STUART WARS

The Highland Charge does not appear to have developed in a recognisable form until during the Great Civil War in the 1640s. The distant origins of that conflict need not detain us since they lay in Edinburgh and London, but the immediate crisis began in Scotland in 1637 with growing resistance to alarmingly arbitrary Royal authority, came to a head with the signing of the famous *National Covenant* in 1638, and developed into a full-blown war between Scotland and England in 1639. By the time both it and the subsequent series of conflicts ended 20 years later, considerable numbers of clansmen had been employed in all three kingdoms of Britain. Within 100 years, their cultural isolation would be ended and the Highlands brought back into the mainstream of Scottish and ultimately British history.

Initially, at least, the employment of Highland troops in the struggle was far from auspicious. As in so many previous wars, the Scots armies which assembled on the border in 1639 and 1640 are known to have included a few small Highland contingents. In the latter year there were, for example, 'some companies of them under Captaine Buchannan and others in Areskine's regiment.' These particular men were evidently *cearnach* armed with bows, rather than larger clan levies, and it is equally clear that they were widely regarded as being no more than rather exotic auxiliaries. Similarly, when an army was raised to go to Ireland in 1642, the Highland regiment levied by the Marquess of Argyll was simply recruited as an irregular light infantry formation, which was reckoned to be capable of pursuing the Irish rebels in bogs and broken ground. It was not envisaged that three years later it would stand in the line of battle at Inverlochy.

In the north-east of Scotland meanwhile, Highlanders were being called out in rather greater numbers to fill the ranks of the Royalist army being raised by the Gordon Marquis of Huntly and his sons. Some, properly equipped with pikes or muskets, served in the regular Strathbogie Regiment, but as many as 500 clansmen from Strathdon and Upper Deeside, under Donald Farquharson of Monaltrie, were present at the battle of Megray Hill on 15 June 1639. By all accounts, this particular group were very poorly armed and were tucked away in the rear. Any doubts which the Royalist leaders may have been harbouring about their reliability were then dramatically borne out when a few cannon-shots sufficed to send them running back, not stopping until they had found refuge in a bog fully half a mile in the rear. By early afternoon, they 'beganne to dropp awaye and marche off in whole companyes' until only a bare handful remained with the army to fight at the Bridge of Dee three days later. It was hardly an encouraging performance.

In short, as a result of the experience of the 'Bishop's War' of 1639, Highlanders were still with some justification held in low esteem by all parties and, unless recruited into regular units, were considered to be of negligible military value, which made what happened next all the more shocking.

It was in Ireland where the real trouble began. King Charles I was desperate to gain allies and as usual he was far from fussy about where he obtained them or what the consequences of employing them might be. His response to the Scots crisis of the 1630s was to plan an ambitious three-pronged offensive which involved an English invasion aimed at Edinburgh, a secondary expedition under the Marquis of Hamilton to reinforce the Scots Royalists in the north-east, and a third force which was to come from Ireland. The latter was to comprise two quite distinct elements; regulars of the Irish standing army under the Earl of Strafford who were to effect a landing in the Clyde valley, and another

much more ominous force of 'volunteers' to be led by Randal McDonnell, Earl of Antrim, which was to land in the western Highlands.

Antrim was a far from prepossessing devil, but in supping with him, King Charles ripped the Highlands apart. Ever since the forfeiture of the Lordship of the Isles in the 15th century, the fortunes of the great Clan Donald had slowly but steadily declined, while those of Clan Diarmeid or Campbell, based in the old Dalriadic heartland of Argyll, just as steadily improved. MacDonald galleys had once controlled the Hebridean seas and the clan held lands in Ulster as well as in Scotland, but by the early 17th century the Campbells held Colonsay and Kintyre and were in a fair way to cutting the old Lordship in half. Antrim therefore saw in the growing conflict between the King and his Scottish subjects a last opportunity for a MacDonald counter-attack.

Nothing came of the planned Irish intervention in 1639 and instead a massive and quite unconnected rebellion broke out there at the end of 1641. Initially the part played in it by the

MacDonalds was an equivocal one. Antrim constantly professed himself a loyal subject, but his people were bound by marriage and sympathy to the O'Cahans and other rebel clans. A further complication was the intervention of a Scots army in Ulster, which included two Campbell regiments and, bizarrely enough, for a time some Colonsay MacDonalds under Coll Coitach's sons. Predictably enough, all the MacDonalds eventually found themselves ranged with the Catholic Confederate rebels, but Antrim himself remained in contact with the King and may have helped broker the 'Cessation' in September 1643. The King primarily entered into this cease-fire in order to bring his own regiments home for the war against his English Parliament, which had begun in 1642, but Antrim also revived the old project of a landing in the western Highlands as a counter to Scots intervention in the English Civil War, and, doubtless to the surprise of all, it finally took place on 8 July 1644.

THE COMING OF THE IRISH

In the end, the vaunted Irish expeditionary force did not amount to very much, comprising rather fewer than 2,000 men in three regiments. The original intention had been to co-ordinate the landing with yet another Royalist uprising in the north-east and a simultaneous cross-border foray by a small Anglo-Scots expeditionary force led by the Marquis of Montrose. Both ventures had ignominiously failed by the time Antrim's men arrived, but a rendezvous with Montrose himself was effected at Blair Atholl on 29 August and the bold decision was taken to mount an offensive towards the city of Perth.

As the King's general, Montrose subsequently claimed all the credit for the victory at Tippermuir which followed on 1 September, but in reality it was won by Antrim's man, Alasdair MacCholla, whose Irish troops executed what is dubiously claimed to have been the first documented

Highlander in belted plaid as depicted by Koler in 1631. Note the ubiquitous 'butcher knife' or rather dirk, omitted in some versions of the print, but slung this time on the right side.

Another, more interesting figure drawn by Koler, this time depicting the old Highland coat, which may have been as common as the belted plaid in the early 17th century, and the eccentric habit of carrying both a bow and quiver, and a matchlock musket.

'Highland Charge' in Scotland.

The battle itself is easily described. Despite Royalist claims to have been outnumbered by around three to one, both armies were in fact pretty well equal in number and were deployed on an open stretch of moorland which offered no real advantage to either side. The government's forces, commanded by Lord Elcho and the Earl of Tullibardine, had some 3,000 infantry, flanked by about 400 cavalry. The Royalists' right wing comprised something in the region of 400 clansmen raised in Atholl, and perhaps as many as another 500 from Badenoch under Ewan Og McPherson, while rather fewer, commanded by Lord Kilpont and MacDonald of Keppoch stood on the left. The centre, commanded by MacCholla, was made up of the three Irish regiments, which after leaving garrisons at Mingarry and Kinlochaline were already down to something like 1,500 men.

It is possible to be reasonably sure just how the Royalists were equipped. For the 400 odd Athollmen, we have the direct evidence of the 1638 *Wapinschaw* returns discussed in the previous chapter, and it is unlikely that the neighbouring Badenoch men differed in the distribution of weapons. There were certainly some bowmen on the left, but although they are casually referred to in secondary sources as belonging to Lord Kilpont's Strathearn Regiment, they must in fact have been Keppoch's people, for Kilpont's men were described by a contemporary as 'armed', which in a 17th century context can only mean that they were properly equipped, with pikes and muskets rather than archaic weapons such as bows.

The same may well have been true of the Irish standing in the Royalist centre. While frequently portrayed as a band of exiled MacDonalds, the composition of the brigade's three regiments, commanded by Colonels Thomas Laghtnan, James MacDonnell and Manus O'Cahan, was actually quite complex and a contemporary diarist named John Spalding, who saw them several times in Aberdeen, described them as 'about 1500 Irishis, brocht up in West Flanderis, expert soldiouris, with ane yeiris pay.' Whilst it is unlikely that all of them were Continental veterans, an examination of the rolls certainly shows them to have in the main been commanded by Irish and Anglo-Irish officers rather than Scots. Many secondary sources also suggest that the soldiers serving in the brigade were armed only with muskets, but there are a number of contemporary references to pikes. George Wishart, Montrose's chaplain cum hagiographer, states that at Tippermuir they were very poorly armed. They had, he says, neither swords nor *long* pikes *(hastis longioribus)* which might be taken to imply that some of them had the half-pikes so common in Irish warfare. There are other casual references to pikes in a number of documents and, in any case, conclusive evidence for the presence of pikemen comes from another contemporary, Patrick Gordon of Ruthven, who relates how one of the Irish regiments saw a slain Royalist officer into his grave with all the usual courtesies including 'trailling of pikes, and thundring vollie of muskets.'

There was nothing conventional about how they fought. Traditionally, the Royalists are said to have marched on to the moor with but a single round apiece and Wishart baldly states that, having driven off Tullibardine's forlorn hope, Montrose ordered the whole army to attack 'with a loud cheer'. As it happens, Wishart's account is then confused by his interpolation of an incident on the right where the poorly armed Athollmen were at one point reduced to throwing stones at the opposing cavalry, and there is considerable doubt as to whether Kilpont and Keppoch advanced at all, but there is no doubting the effectiveness of the Irish attack in the centre. Briskly marching up to Tullibardine's men, they fired a single volley and then fell on them with pike, dirk and musket-butt, routing them completely and initiating a bloody pursuit which stretched all the way to the gates of Perth.

This, it has been suggested, was the genesis of the Highland Charge, although MacCholla had reportedly employed it for the first time in a battle on the Laney two years before. At the battle of Naseby in 1645, the English Royalist army was to employ exactly the same tactics, as the King's secretary, Edward Walker famously related: 'Presently our Forces advanced up the Hill, the Rebels only discharging five Pieces at them, but over shot them, and so did their Musquetiers. The Foot on either side hardly saw each other until they were with Carabine Shot, and so only made one Volley; ours falling on with Sword and butt end of Musquet did notable Execution so much as I saw their Colours fall and their Foot in great Disorder.' There is other evidence that this particular attack at Naseby was a far from

isolated incident and, while the Irish example may have had some influence on the development of the Highland Charge, its full flowering still lay in the future.

Consequently, the battle of Inverlochy, fought at Candlemass, 2 February 1645, is perhaps a more interesting action. Despite the completeness of the victory at Tippermuir, Montrose recognised that his army was far too small to contemplate an immediate advance on Edinburgh and so he turned instead for the north-east. There, he hoped to be able to persuade the Gordons to rise once again for the King, but instead found himself fighting another full-scale battle against some local levies under Lord Balfour of Burleigh at the Justice Mills, outside Aberdeen two weeks later on 14 September. Although he had by then been joined by a handful of cavalry, his only infantry belonged to the three Irish regiments and this

The old Brig of Dee, Aberdeen, scene of a two-day battle in 1639. The bridge itself was held by the Aberdeen Militia, but Highlanders of the Strathbogie Regiment, commanded by the infamous Nathaniel Gordon, occupied the riverbank in the foreground.

time they were engaged in a prolonged and inconclusive firefight before Montrose ordered Laghtnan's regiment to 'lay aside their Muskets and Pikes, and fall on with Sword and Durk'. Burleigh's infantry broke and once again something of a massacre ensued, which not only alienated potential supporters but reinforced the notion that Montrose's men were a peculiarly savage and barbaric lot. Since that battle, the Royalist army had not been engaged in any substantial fighting, but on MacCholla's insistence, a midwinter invasion of Argyllshire for the first time brought in substantial reinforcements from the western clans.

The end of January found Montrose halfway up the Great Glen at Kilchummin (now Fort Augustus) and aware that an army under the Mackenzie Earl of Seaforth was gathering to oppose him at Inverness. Of itself this intelligence was not particularly worrying, but then came

word that the Marquess of Argyll had belatedly mobilised the 'power' of Clan Campbell to pursue the Royalists and avenge the sacking of Inverary at Christmas. He was now arrived at Inverlochy and both ends of the Great Glen were thus blocked. Although there was still nothing to prevent the Royalists escaping eastwards into Stratherrick or even Strathspey, Montrose was once again pressured by MacCholla into turning south to Inverlochy and a bloody clash in the snow between Clan Campbell and Clan Donald, which had nothing to do with King or Covenant and everything to do with ancient rivalries.

Having taken the decision to fight, the Royalists embarked on an ambitious flank march, first climbing due south up Glen Tarff as far as Culachy and then into Glen Buck, shielded from Campbell scouts by the long ridges of Meall a Cholumain and Druim Laragan. By now, they were 1,000 feet up and had a further 1,000 feet to

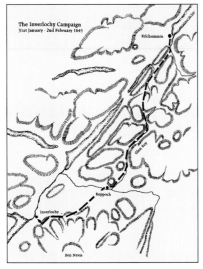

The Inverlochy Campaign
31st January - 2nd February 1645

Kilchummin

Glen Roy

Keppoch

Inverlochy

Ben Nevis

Left, Inverlochy.

Above, the banners of the King in Glen Roy. English Civil War Society re-enactors recreate Montrose and MacCholla's epic march from Kilchummin to Inverlochy. Carn na Larach is in the background and there is a notable lack of snow.

climb in order to reach the col beneath Carn na Larach and pass out on to the windswept Teanga Plateau. From there, the going was much easier as they descended first into Glen Turret and then Glen Roy, before reaching the Spean at Keppoch. There, for the first time, they encountered a hostile patrol and halted at the farm for about three hours while the army closed up and, long after darkness had fallen, took up a position at Torlundy, overlooking Argyll's forces at Inverlochy. In just 36 hours, they had marched 50 kilometres over the hills in midwinter and were now about to fight an army reported to be twice their number.

SLAUGHTER IN THE SNOW

The Royalists had only some 1,500 men, organised in four 'divisions' or battalions. Alasdair MacCholla took command of the right wing at the head of Laghtnan's Irish regiment, while the left comprised another Irish regiment under Colonel O'Cahan. Neither can have been much more than 300 or 400 strong. In the centre, for the first time, there was a fairly substantial body of Highlanders; some 500 MacDonalds, Macleans, Appin Stewarts and, perhaps, Athollmen as well in the front line, which in all conscience is a remarkably small body of men, considering it was made up of at least four clan contingents. Even if, as seems likely, the Athollmen formed a reserve with the third Irish regiment under Colonel James MacDonnell, this can only represent a 'select band' of gentlemen and *cearnach*, rather than the full power of these clans, *ghillies* and all.

For his part, Argyll prudently remained aboard his personal galley, leaving his army to be drawn up by an experienced professional soldier, Sir Duncan Campbell of Auchinbreck. Oddly enough, his dispositions largely mirrored those of the Royalists. He too placed his regulars, 16 companies of infantry largely drawn from the Earl of Moray's and Tullibardine's Regiments, on the wings and formed his Highlanders in the

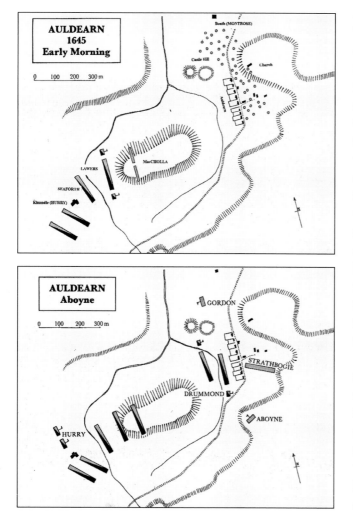

Top, shortly after dawn, MacCholla has taken up a position on the low hill east of Auldearn with his Lifeguard and William Gordon of Monymore's Highlanders. Sir Mungo Campbell of Lawers' regulars, supported by Seaforth's Mackenzies, is advancing into contact.

Bottom, Aboyne's regular cavalry begin the Royalist counter-attack by moving in on Major Drummond's troop of horse. The rest of the Royalist cavalry under Lord Gordon are north of the Castle Hill and the Strathbogie Regiment has been mustered east of the village.

centre, in a field known as the *Goitean Odhar*. According to Gordon of Ruthven, there was a strong battalion posted a little way in front of the main body, well armed with guns, bows and axes, which was presumably the regiment which Argyll had raised for the Irish service in 1642 as Auchinbreck was its actual commander. Such a particular description of their arms clearly implies that the men standing behind them were rather less well equipped, as might be expected given that this was a general levying out of the Clan Campbell.

The battle began at dawn and the Irish regiments on the wings followed their usual practice of marching straight up to the opposing regular battalions, fired a single volley 'which fyred their beards' and then fell on briskly. Staggered by this display of naked aggression, the regulars promptly broke and ran. Having thus secured his flanks, Montrose then ordered his centre to advance with equal success. In outline what happened is straightforward enough. Argyll's Regiment, the battalion mentioned by Ruthven, fired a single volley at the oncoming Highlanders, then fell back in confusion on the half-armed *ghillies* standing in their rear. Almost at once, the whole lot dissolved into a panic-stricken mob which was incapable of offering any resistance, and hundreds are said to have been killed in the subsequent pursuit. On the face of it, the battle would appear to offer a textbook example of the Highland Charge in action, but curiously little attention has been paid to the way in which the Campbell levies, gentlemen, *cearnach* and *ghillies,* together stood on the defensive rather than launching a charge of their own. This argues for a certain conservatism on the Campbells' part as they tried to fight in the traditional fashion, in which the gentlemen expected to engage in mortal combat with their equals while the *ghillies* backed them up.

Although there is an easy assumption that the

Top, the Castle Hill, Auldearn, as seen from Campbell of Lawers' position. The hill was occupied by William Gordon of Monymore's Regiment while MacCholla was holding the village.

Bottom, the old village street, Auldearn, looking north. The buildings post-date the battle but give a good idea of scale and the low-lying situation of the village in 1645. The modern one now chiefly lies along an east-west axis.

Royalists' success was due to their launching a full-blooded Highland Charge, it is perhaps questionable whether this was in fact the case, or whether it was the turning of Auchinbreck's flanks which caused the initial panic, after which the poorly armed Campbell *ghillies* can have been no match for the Royalist swordsmen. Iain Lom, the Bard of Keppoch, exulted over the slaughter:

'The most pleasing news every time it was announced about the wry-mouthed Campbells, was that every company of them as they came along had their heads battered with sword blows.

'Were you familiar with the *Goirtean Odhar*? Well was it manured, not with the dung of sheep or goats, But by the blood of Campbells after it had congealed.

'Perdition take you if I feel pity for your plight, As I listen to the distress of your children, Lamenting the company which was in the battlefield, The wailing of the women of Argyll.'

The other results of the victory at Inverlochy were curiously mixed. Inverness and its regular garrison was left well alone, and the Royalists passed into Speyside where they were briefly joined by James Grant of Freuchie, the Laird of Grant. Then they turned north for Elgin, where a regular cavalry regiment commanded by Lord Gordon defected and precipitated something of an avalanche of politic submissions headed by the Earl of Seaforth. Encouraged by this, if not by the mere handful of genuine recruits who trickled in, the Royalists then embarked upon what can only be described as a great *chevauchee* or foray through the north-east, with decidedly patchy results. Farquharson of Monaltrie was killed in a squalid little affair in Aberdeen and eventually it culminated in a badly bungled raid on Dundee and an undignified flight into the hills. With the road to the north temporarily clear, one of the government's more experienced officers,

Recreated Highland clansman with matchlock musket, evidently a *ghillie* as he lacks a broadsword or any other military equipment.

Sir John Hurry, embarked on a sweep of his own, aimed at a rendezvous with Seaforth and the other northern leaders at Inverness.

Not surprisingly, the Royalists quickly emerged again in pursuit, which was exactly what Hurry wanted. Crossing the Spey on 3 May, he then conducted a skilful rearguard action as he steadily approached Inverness and the promised reinforcements. By the 7th, Montrose had outstripped his infantry in his eagerness to close with Hurry and was getting dangerously near Inverness. At this point, he called it a day, broke contact and fell back to a concentration area in and around the village of Auldearn, a few miles east of Nairn. Unfortunately the term 'concentration' proved to be something of a misnomer, for when Hurry, linking up with Seaforth next day, turned around and attacked at dawn on the 9th, he found the Royalists very 'commodiously' encamped.

Having apparently caught them napping, Hurry decided to mount a hasty assault on the village with the intention of defeating the scattered detachments in detail. Some scouts sent out by MacCholla provided a vital few minutes' warning and he and his Lifeguard moved out to meet Hurry's advance with the first of a series of spoiling attacks, while Montrose hastily rallied the army. In MacCholla's desperate struggle first to delay Hurry and then to hold the village, we are provided with a last, vivid glimpse of the old heroic style of Highland warfare, in which everything hinged on individual prowess rather than the massed rush of what was to become the Highland Charge.

THE VALIANT ALASDAIR

There is no doubt that Hurry's forces hastening up the road and deploying along the Auldearn burn at Kinnudie, as they heard the Royalist drums frantically beating to arms, were considerably stronger than their opponents.

He had some 300 cavalry and no fewer than five regiments or at least detachments of regular infantry, totalling something in the region of 1,600 well-trained men, and in addition there were as many more raised out of the northern clans under Seaforth, Sutherland and Lovat. The Royalists, on the other hand, may have had about the same number of cavalry under Lord Gordon, but only, according to Montrose himself, 1,400 foot, comprising the Irish (now forming just one battalion), and two Gordon battalions, the old Strathbogie Regiment and a newly raised one from Strathavan commanded by William Gordon of Monymore. When the battle began, Alasdair MacCholla could only actually count upon the 140 men of his own Lifeguard and about 200 more belonging to Monymore's Regiment.

Instead of standing on the defensive in the village, MacCholla led his men westwards 'towards a marishe and som bushes, which was a strong ground and fencible against horsemen.' This position can be identified as a low rise more or less surrounded by the Auldearn Burn and it is important to appreciate that low as the hill was, it very effectively masked the main Royalist position from view by Hurry and his army at Kinnudie. Not surprisingly, therefore, Hurry began by sending one of his regular units, probably Sir Mungo Campbell of Lawers', against MacCholla. The Royalists opened fire first but were badly outnumbered and, according to one of the northern levies named James Fraser, MacCholla's own Ensign was shot down in the first volley. His yellow banner was raised again at once, but no fewer than three or four men holding it were shot down in quick succession before he conceded defeat and 'efter a brave and long maintained resistance, he is forced to reteir to som yards of the town.'

Lawers' Regiment, supported by Seaforth's levies, followed them up, but MacCholla made a stand in the backyards, before attempting another

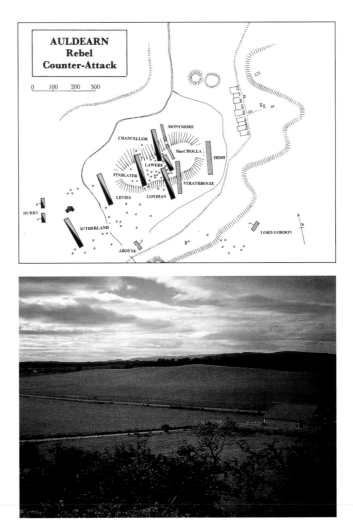

Top, while the Royalist cavalry rally on the southern fringes of the battlefield, the Royalist infantry push westwards along the low hill. Hurry's regulars are giving way under the pressure and no attempt has been made to commit the northern levies.

Bottom, the Auldearn battlefield as seen from the Castle Hill. The low hill was the scene of most of the fighting.

spoiling attack. This very quickly came to grief and soon they were fighting hand to hand amongst the houses and yards. During the retreat from Dundee in April, MacCholla's servant had been captured while carrying his master's hat, cloak and gloves, but that morning at Auldearn it was not a fine gentleman but a Gaelic warlord who held Lawers' men at bay: 'He was ever in the front, and his strenth, his curage, and dexteritie let his enemies sie, even with terror, wonderful feates of armes for his fellowes to imitate, his strong arme cutting asunder whatsoever or whosoever did him resist. He brack two swords: and whan they had fastened a number of pikes in his tairge, wherwith they could have born thre or four ordinarie men to the ground, they could not make him to shrink, or bow so much as ane kne to the ground; but with a blow of his sword the strenth of his vallorous arme cute all the pikes asunder that stuck in his target, whill non durst approach within the lenth of his weappon.'

The story told by McMuirich and other MacDonald chroniclers is even more dramatic. When his second sword was broken, Alasdair was handed a third by his brother-in-law, who was himself cut down before he could regain the doubtful security of one of the houses. As MacCholla fell back, he was covered by another of his men, Ranald MacDomniull, who pistolled an advancing pikeman only to have one of Seaforth's Lewismen shoot an arrow through both cheeks. Dropping the empty pistol, Ranald then tried to draw his sword, only to find it had stuck in the scabbard. Unable to protect himself, he also received a number of pike wounds before he eventually dragged it out and ran to the nearest house, where he could hear Alasdair loudly cursing his reluctant Gordon allies. One of the pikemen followed close behind, only to have his head cut off by MacCholla as soon as he stuck it through the door. By now Alasdair and his Lifeguard had given themselves up for lost,

but there was no thought of retreating: 'Alasdair... you were good that day at Auldearn, when you leapt among the pikes; and whether good or ill befell you, you would not shout Relief'.

The fight for the village was absorbing all of Hurry's attention. Not only had his offensive become bogged down, but he still had properly to deploy his army. Unaware of Montrose's actual position, his regiments were simply stacked up behind the action and consequently horribly vulnerable when the Royalist counter-attack eventually came in. This occurred in two distinct phases. First Lord Gordon's regiment, divided into two squadrons commanded by himself and by his brother Viscount Aboyne, attacked both flanks of Lawers' brigade more or less simultaneously. Their troopers were not the rude multitude of 'bonnet lairds on cart-horses' imagined by John Buchan, but regulars and they proceeded to demonstrate the fact by routing Lawers' men in short order. The rest of Hurry's army still remained unengaged, but now, to his palpable horror, James Fraser saw the Strathbogie Regiment sweeping around the south side of Auldearn and then driving westwards to engage the next brigade comprising Lothian's and the Lord Chancellor's regiments. Montrose himself noted in his subsequent dispatch to the King that there were 'some hot salvyes of musket and a litell dealing with sword and pike' (which hardly suggests an undisciplined charge), but Fraser only remembered how the rebels 'run throw them, killing and goaring under foot... Lairs [sic] and Lothians regiment stood in their ranks and files, and were so killed as they stood", while Ruthven, a Royalist eyewitness, rather more exultantly wrote 'you should have sein how the infantrie of the Royalists, keiping together and following the charge of the horsemen, did tear and cut them in pieces, even in rankes and fyles, as they stood, so great was the execution, which they made efter the horse had shaken and quyt astonished

Highland musketeer after Koler. It is possible that he is wearing tartan breeches but it seems likelier that they are badly drawn trews. The bonnet may also be made of tartan material.

them, by persueing rudely throw them, as it was very lamentable to behold.'

As usual, the defeat of the regulars precipitated a general collapse and a furious pursuit in which the northern Highlanders suffered as heavily as any. Captain Bernard Mackenzie was killed together with most of his company from the Chanonry of Ross, as was Robert Grant, a son of Shueglie, and Fraser records that Lovat was left with no fewer than 87 Fraser widows to support.

There is no doubting that Auldearn was a bloody, brutal business, which may have lasted all day, for Hurry claimed to have got away under cover of darkness, but the part played in it by the hundreds of Highlanders present on both sides was curiously muted. Most were armed with pike, musket or bow and the struggle was grim rather than spectacular, but the Gaelic bards such as Iain Lom were in no doubt as to where the real credit should go: 'Health and joy to the valiant Alasdair who won the battle of Auldearn with his army; You were not a feeble poltroon engaging in the crossing of swords when you were in the enclosure alone. Helmeted men with pikes in their hands were attacking you with all their might until you were relieved by Montrose.'

The Royalists too had suffered heavily in the battle, losing according to Gordon of Sallagh, 22 'gentlemen' and 200 common soldiers. Instead of following up his victory by moving on Inverness, Montrose retreated eastwards across the Spey, only to find himself pursued by another army, this time led by William Baillie. In an exhausting series of marches and counter-marches, the 'Auld Dog' caught the Royalists at Alford in Aberdeenshire on 2 July 1645 with six regiments of foot totalling no more than 1,400 men, and about 300 cavalry. The composition of Montrose's army drawn up on the Gallows Hill is not entirely clear, though he certainly outnumbered Baillie, with at least 2,000 foot and 200 horse. As usual, Lord Gordon's Regiment was divided between the two wings

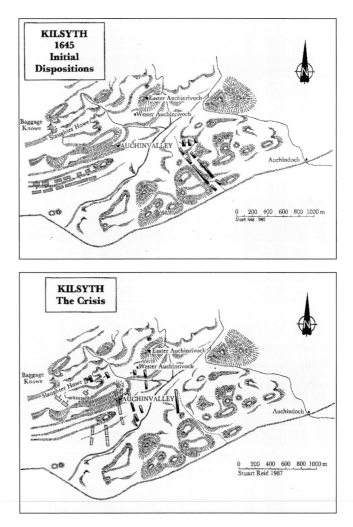

Top, the Royalist army is drawn up on the hillside overlooking the Glasgow road, unaware that William Baillie is deploying on their left flank.

Bottom, An extremely confused battle is in progress as the Royalists desperately respond to Baillie's disorganised offensive. Both generals have lost control.

and backed up by the Irish regiments, while Ruthven specifically mentions that the main battle comprised the Strathbogie Regiment (probably commanded by John Gordon of Littlemill), and 'Huntly's highlanders', that is, Monymore's Strathavan regiment and a Deeside battalion under Farquharson of Inverey. Wishart, ever anxious to play down the Gordon contribution, claims that the centre was commanded by Glengarry, which would at least argue for the presence of a small MacDonald contingent. The battle itself was a straightforward affair, once again a brutal slogging match, rather than a dramatic avalanche of steel down the slopes of the Gallows Hill, and in the end it was won by the Royalist cavalry, who first beat the troopers opposite them and then turned on Baillie's infantry. Outnumbered as they were, Baillie had been forced to draw them up only three deep and now he had to pronounce their grim epitaph: 'Our foot stood with myselfe and behaved themselves as became them, untill the enemies horse charged in our reare, and in front we were overcharged with their foot.'

TRIUMPH OF THE WESTERN CLANS

Alasdair MacCholla had missed the battle, but when he rendezvoused with Montrose at Fordoun in the Mearns, he brought in no fewer than 1,400 men of the western clans and another 200 Athollmen under Patrick Graham of Inchbrackie. It was a significant moment in Highland history and one which was to have far-reaching consequences. Montrose had of course employed Highlanders before, but thus far they had very largely been fighting on their home ground. Now for the first time since Harlaw in 1411, a predominantly Highland army was marching deep into the Lowlands.

Baillie tried to stop them at Bridge of Earn, but they bypassed his fortified camp and pushed southwards, crossing the Forth for the first time and bringing him across Stirling Bridge in pursuit. From Stirling, he marched to Denny and there established that the Royalists were encamped at Kilsyth on a high meadow overlooking the Glasgow road. Next day, he was ordered by his political masters to attack, but mindful of the dangers of continuing down the road, 'marched with the regiments through the corns and over the braes, untill the impassible ground did hold us up. There I imbattled, where I doubt if on any quarter twenty men on a front could either have gone from us or attacked us.'

So far so good, and even the must cursory examination of the ground today bears out Baillie's remarks. It was no place to fight a battle and as a further advance upon the present line was impossible, Baillie was persuaded to shift towards some high ground to his right occupied by the farms of Easter and Wester Auchinrivoch. Despite what is said in all too many secondary sources, the move itself presented no danger since Baillie's regiments were initially lying on a reverse slope, hidden from the Royalists' view.

They for their part had drawn up in order of battle on the meadow, overlooking the road which they rather too confidently expected Baillie to come marching down, and at first were quite unaware that he was in fact turning their flank. Then, when his advance guard began racing towards Wester Auchinrivoch, all hell broke loose.

According to his very detailed post-action report presented to the subsequent court of inquiry, Baillie had just five regiments of regulars under his command: the Marquis of Argyll's (not to be confused with his Highland regiment destroyed at Inverlochy), the Earl of Crawford-Lindsay's, Colonel Robert Home's Redcoats, the Earl of Lauderdale's and 'three that were joyned in one', the last being the remnants of units which had earlier been badly cut up at Auldearn and Alford. In addition to these veterans, there was a brigade of three newly levied regiments from Fife:

Cameron colour still preserved at Achnacarry. The arm and sword crest, rather than Locheil's bundle of arrows identifies this as Cameron of Glendessary's 'ruddy banner' seen by Almerieclose at Dalcomera in 1689.

Opposite, a useful rear view by McIan, showing the belted plaid used as a cloak.

R R McIan

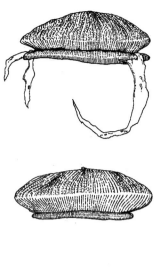

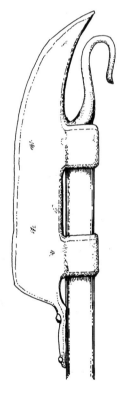

Morton's, Arnott's and Henderson's. In total, he must have had something in the region of 3,000 or 3,500 infantry, together with three cannon, including one nicknamed *Prince Robert* which had been captured at Marston Moor, and the extremely low total of 360 cavalry under the Earl of Balcarres.

The Royalists on the other hand equalled him in foot and, surprisingly enough, outnumbered him by nearly two to one in cavalry. Interestingly, only about a third of their infantry were regulars belonging to the Strathbogie Regiment, and what was left of the Irish Brigade. The rest were Highlanders; the Western Clans, the Athollmen, the Farquharsons under Inverey and Gordon of Monymore's Strathavan Regiment. It is difficult to be very precise about how they were actually drawn up, since a certain amount of confusion was reigning in the Royalist camp as they hurriedly strove to re-align themselves to face Baillie's flanking attack, but he reckoned to have been initially facing Highlanders rather than regulars.

At any rate, he was in no doubt as to the sequence of events which precipitated the battle. At the commencement of the operation, he detached a body of regular musketeers under Major John Haldane of the Lord Chancellor's Regiment to act as an advance guard, but seeing a party of Highlanders led by Captain Ewan MacLean of Treshnish filtering into the enclosures at Auchinvalley, Haldane immediately attacked them instead of pressing on to Auchinrivoch. Baillie promptly sent two officers to recall him in quick succession, but it was too late, for first Glengarry came hurrying up to reinforce Treshnish with his MacDonalds, and then MacCholla came after him with the rest of the western clans.

The battle was fast attaining a momentum of its own and Baillie, 'seeing the rebels fall up strong I desired them [the committee] to retire,

and the officers to goe to their charge. My Lord Balcarras and I galloped back to the regiments. He asked me what he should doe? I desired him to draw up his regiment on the right hand of the Earl of Lauderdale's. I gave order to Lauderdale's both by myselfe and my adjutant, to face to the right hand, and to march to the foot of the hill, then to face as they were; to Hume to follow their steps, halt when they halted, and keep distance and front with them. The Marquess his Major, as I went toward him, asked what he should doe? I told him, he should draw up on Hume's left hand, as he had done before. I had not ridden farr from him, when looking back, I find Hume had left the way I put him in, and wes gone at a trott, right west, in among the dykes and toward the enemy.'

Hume's sudden offensive succeeded in relieving Haldane and established a lodgement in the nearer enclosure, supported by the two other regiments which had followed in his wake, but the Royalists were throwing in more and more men as fast as they could be turned around and marched to the sound of the guns, while Baillie was desperately trying to regain control: 'I followed alse fast as I could ride, and meeting the Adjutant on the way, desired him he should bring up the Earl of Crafurd's regiment to Lauderdale's left hand, and cause the Generall-Major [John] Leslie draw up the regiments of Fyfe in reserve as of before, but before I could come to Hume, he and the other two regiments, to wit, the Marquess of Argyles and the three that were joyned in one, had taken in an enclosure, from whilk, the enemy being so neer, it wes impossible to bring them off.'

For a time, the situation was stabilised. Baillie's regulars were esconced behind stone walls and blazing away like mad at the Highlanders, who far from rushing upon them sword in hand, were sheltering behind the dykes on the other side of the enclosure. Now it was the cavalry's turn, and at first Balcarres' troopers held their ground, but once again more and more Royalist units were fed

Top, 17th century knitted bonnets from Dava Moor, Cromdale (top), Tarvie, Ross-shire and Quintfall Hill, Caithness. The Tarvie bonnet looks remarkably like those depicted by Koler in 1631.
Bottom, the Lochaber Axe was much cheaper and easier to manufacture than the gentleman's broadsword. In October 1715, the burgh of Aberdeen was ordered to make up 300 and send them to the Jacobite camp at Perth for the arming of recruits.

piecemeal into the fight until sheer weight of numbers prevailed. As at Alford, once Balcarres' men were driven back, the Royalist cavalry turned on the rear of the beleaguered infantry and this was the signal for the Highlanders to come forward again. 'In the end,' remembered Baillie, 'the rebells leapt over the dyke, and with downe heads fell on and broke these regiments.'

This was the beginning of the end. As his regulars gave way, Baillie looked to the reserves, but the Fife levies were already running and after a final attempt to rally his broken foot near Auchincloch, he fled to Stirling. Behind him he left a bloody massacre. As is often the way of it, his regulars, although well battered, do seem to have escaped reasonably intact, but the exultant clansmen pursued the fleeing Fifers for miles, mercilessly cutting them down. While their exact losses can never be known, it is said that a whole generation was wiped out in many villages and that boats were left to rot at their moorings in the East Neuk ports for want of men to sail them.

Ultimately, Kilsyth turned out to be a hollow victory for the Royalists since Montrose failed to hold his army together afterwards and, at the beginning of September, Alasdair MacCholla marched off with the western clans. Montrose, making a doomed attempt to link up with the King, was defeated by David Leslie at Philiphaugh on 13 September 1645, and although he retrieved a few hundred men from the disaster and kept going until the general surrender in the following year, he was no longer a threat. Similarly, MacCholla's attempt to re-establish a MacDonald hegemony in the west also crumbled with surprising speed. By June 1647, he was back in Ireland and died in battle shortly afterwards.

Despite the prominent part played by the clans in these campaigns and more particularly at Kilsyth, Leslie and the other Scots commanders would probably still have agreed with Henry Hawley in regarding Highlanders as 'the most

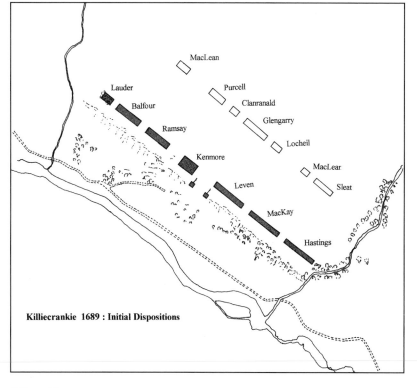

Killiecrankie 1689 : Initial Dispositions

Killiecrankie

despicable enemie that are'. In early 1647, the regular Scots army was 'New Modelled' and two of the seven infantry units authorised on the new establishment; Argyll's and Campbell of Ardkinglas's, were Highland units. They were not to be employed as shock troops, but rather employed in a counter-insurgency role in the hills. The only other concession to the perils of Highland warfare was the establishment of a detachment of 70 armoured halberdiers in each regular infantry unit. No reason was given at the time for this decree, but during the Jacobite War of 1689 similar detachments were deployed as piquets forward of each regiment when operating in 'Indian country.'

While a superficial reading of these events might point to the successful advent of the famous Highland Charge, a more careful study suggests a less dramatic interpretation. There is no question that when Highlanders were engaged, on the Royalist side at least, they closed with the enemy at a run, that they did indeed charge. However, those charges were the culminating act of battles which were otherwise fought in a more conventional fashion, rather than the principal one upon which the outcome of the battle depended.

In a very real sense, the groundwork for the classic Highland Charge was well and truly laid during the Civil War years, for the psychological impact of Highland intervention was deep and far reaching. Both north and south of the border, the Civil War came as the culmination of years of political rather than violent conflict. Writing in 1626, Sir Edward Cecil grumblingly commented that 'This Kingdom [England] hath been too long at peace – our old commanders both by sea and by land are worn out, and few men are bred in their places, for the knowledge of war and almost the thought of war is extinguished.' This was equally true north of the border. While a certain degree of violence might have been endemic in

the Highlands, the rest of Scotland was as accustomed to peace and more or less civilised behaviour as its English neighbour. Large scale warfare and all its attendant horrors was something which happened far away, in Germany or the Low Countries. Even after 1642, the war in England was, except for a few isolated incidents, very much a civil war conducted with the behaviour to be expected from men who knew that when it was over they would have to live as neighbours once again. In Scotland by contrast, MacCholla and Montrose began and proceeded with unprecedented savagery. Each victory was followed by a ruthless massacre of fugitives and all too often innocent civilians as well, culminating in the awful slaughter of the Fife regiments at Kilsyth. Highlanders had well and truly emerged from their post-Harlaw obscurity to establish a terrible reputation for ruthlessness and cruelty.

THE JACOBITE WAR

The Highlanders' terrible reputation was exploited with considerable effect in 1689. When John Graham of Claverhouse—alias 'Bluidy Claver'rse' or 'Bonnie Dundee', according to political persuasion—raised the first Jacobite standard at Dalcomera, he did so at the head of a Highland army. Consequently, the battle of Killiecrankie affords the first real example of such an army in action since Harlaw.

The campaign began on 4 April 1689, with a declaration by the Scots government that the deeply unpopular King James VII had 'forfaultit the Croun' and the subsequent offer of it to his daughter Mary and her husband, William of Orange. James still had his supporters, but they were outnumbered and politically outmanoeuvred. With little chance of rallying an army in the Lowlands, Claverhouse rode north into the Highlands and called for a great gathering at Dalcomera on 18 May. The response was encouraging, but little was achieved until July

Opposite, the 'Young Pretender', Prince Charles Edward Stuart, as depicted by McIan. Although a popular image, the Prince normally wore *truibhs* and does not appear to have worn a kilt or plaid until he was on the run after Culloden.

Top, The titular King James VIII of Scotland and III of England. Born in 1688, he was the "Old Pretender" and successive Jacobite uprisings in 1715, 1719 and 1745 were launched in his name.

Bottom, Colour carried by John Gordon of Glenbuchat's Regiment in 1745. The presence of a coronet above the Gordon arms suggests that it may originally have been carried by Huntly's Regiment in 1715 – Glenbuchat was then its Lieutenant Colonel.

when the new Commander-in-Chief in Scotland, a Highlander named Hugh Mackay of Scourie, decided to come looking for him.

Mackay's original intention was to march directly to Inverlochy, rendezvous with local forces being raised by Argyll and then proceed from there, but hearing that Stewart of Ballechin had gone over to the rebels and seized Blair Castle, he changed his plans and decided to clear the Inverness road first. Unknown to him, Claverhouse had at the same time received word that the powerful Earl of Breadalbane (a Campbell) had finally decided to support King James after all. As a result, he too set his men marching for Blair, although neither general was to be aware for some days that their armies were on a collision course.

On 25 July, Mackay left Stirling at the head of six regiments of foot, all but one of them Scots, and two troops of militia horse. Next day at Dunkeld, he received a worried note from Lord Murray, the Marquis of Atholl's son, advising him that the Jacobites were moving south, although the Pass of Killiecrankie was still open. Undeterred, Mackay responded by ordering Murray to hold the Pass until Lieutenant Colonel George Lauder could come to his aid with 200 picked grenadiers. At dawn, on the morning of

the 27th, Lauder found Murray gone and the Pass unguarded, but pushed through it and took up a position at the north end. Marching after him, Mackay entered the Pass at noon and four hours later had his whole army safely through. By this time, Lauder's grenadiers, safely esconced on a small wooded hillock by Aldclune, had a good view of some scattered parties of men advancing towards them. Mackay came up to have a look for himself and not unnaturally concluded that it was Claverhouse's advance guard, but the Jacobite leader, in fact, was engaged in an ambitious attempt to outflank him.

Instead of pushing straight down the road, Claverhouse had fetched a compass around the north of the Hill of Lude and even as Mackay watched he began drawing up his army on the south face of Greag Eallich, a steep hill overlooking the mouth of the Pass. He may indeed have hoped to catch the soldiers as they debouched from it, but instead Mackay took immediate steps to meet the assault. His army was still stretched out along the road from Aldclune to the Pass, and Colonel Ferdinando Hastings' Regiment, the only English unit, had not yet cleared it. Facing to the right, Mackay's men were confronted by a fairly 'steep and difficult ascent' covered with trees and shrubs, rising to just above the 100 metre contour line and a broad terrace known as the Urrard plateau. It would clearly have been foolish to remain on the road facing this wooded slope immediately to their front and so Mackay marched his 3,500 infantry up on to the plateau and deployed them in order of battle. Lauder's grenadiers, in the birch wood at Aldclune, covered his left flank, and next to them, stood Colonel Bartholomew Balfour's Regiment, drawn up in two battalions, and then Colonel George Ramsay's. Both regiments, forming a brigade under Balfour, were drawn up in three ranks in order to maximise their firepower, but were separated from the next regiment in line,

Viscount Kenmore's, by a bog which may have been as much as 100 metres across. This turned out to be particularly unfortunate for Kenmore's Regiment, which had only been raised in April, for some reason remaining drawn up six ranks deep instead of forming three like everybody else. Consequently, there was a substantial gap between its right flank and the next three regiments in line, the Earl of Leven's, Mackay's and Hastings'. The gap was partially covered by three light artillery pieces and the two militia cavalry troops raised by Lord Belhaven and the Earl of Annandale, but to all intents and purposes Kenmore's Regiment, perhaps the least reliable unit in Mackay's army, was standing alone, isolated in the very centre of the line.

Deploying along a much narrower terrace up by the steadings at Orchil and Lettoch, the Jacobite army was drawn up in three distinct bodies with a strong centre and two rather weaker wings separated from it by as much as 200 metres on either side. This arrangement was far from ideal, but Claverhouse had no alternative if his 2,500 men were not to be outflanked. The body forming the right wing was Sir John Maclean's Regiment, while the left was formed by Sir Donald MacDonald of Sleat's Regiment and Sir Allan Maclean's Regiment. As to the centre, it included

Sir James Purcell's white-coated Irish regiment, the MacDonalds of Clanranald and Glengarry (who as usual included the Glencoe men, the Glen Urquhart and Glenmoriston Grants), the Stewarts of Appin and Sir Ewen Cameron of Locheil's Regiment.

Claverhouse's own little troop of horse and the 300-odd men serving in Purcell's Regiment have some claim to being regulars, as, oddly enough do Sir Allan Maclean's men, for his 200-strong regiment was recruited from a number of different clans, stiffened by two Irish companies and generally reckoned on all sides to be the toughest in the army. Otherwise, this was a Highland host, largely if not entirely made up of gentlemen and *cearnach*, or so it may be inferred from the fact that the individual regimental totals were well down on the figures achieved by the same clans in 1745-46, when it is known that the *ghillies* were levied out as well. At one point Claverhouse had tried to persuade Locheil to have his men trained as 'proper' soldiers and, although the regular Highland battalions which were to serve Dutch William on other battlefields show that it could have been done, Locheil refused on the grounds that they lacked both the arms and ammunition which would have been necessary. He may well have been right in the circumstances,

This aggressive looking left-handed individual is identified by the Penicuik artist as Glengarry, presumably Alexander McDonnell, younger of Glengarry, who was accidentally shot and killed after the battle of Falkirk.

A rather portly Highland gentleman and his retainer. Although the original sketch is not identified, this may well be Charles Stewart of Ardsheal, commander of the Appin Regiment.

but his refusal led directly to the way in which the battle would be fought and so nearly lost. In short, unable to engage in a firefight, the only tactic open to the Jacobites was a headlong rush towards the enemy at the earliest opportunity.

KILLIECRANKIE

Once drawn up, neither side at first showed much enthusiasm for closing with the other. Naturally enough, there was no question of Mackay and his men embarking upon a mountaineering expedition, while the Jacobites seem to have been rather preoccupied with counting heads and coming up with the unpalatable conclusion that they were badly outnumbered and outgunned. Taking comfort from this, Mackay successfully provoked a forward movement by ordering his master gunner, James Smith, to open fire. The three little 'leather' guns proved to be ineffective weapons, but in response to the brief cannonade (cut short when the flimsy gun carriages 'broke with the third firing'), a party of Camerons tried to occupy a couple of cottages to their immediate front. A party of musketeers from Mackay's Regiment then advanced in turn and drove them back, whereupon Claverhouse, anxious that this minor reverse should not be taken as a bad omen, waved his army forward and at about eight o'clock in the evening, the Highlanders set off down the steep slope and into a ferocious storm of fire.

It is easy to describe Killiecrankie very simply and General Wade may have had the battle in mind when he penned his own handy guide to Highland warfare: 'When in sight of the Enemy they endeavour to possess themselves of the highest Ground, believing they descend on them with greater force. They generally give their fire at a distance, they lay down their Arms [i.e., firelocks] on the Ground and make a Vigorous attack with their Broad swords, but if repulsed, seldom or never rally again.' In the very broadest terms, this was exactly what happened. Claverhouse and his

Highlanders came down the steep slope of Creag Eallaich, fired a volley, charged and swept away Mackay's army in a matter of minutes. On closer examination, a more complex picture emerges which at the same time provides a very useful explanation of how the phenomenon called the Highland Charge actually worked.

Far from being completely swept away, Mackay's line was initially penetrated at only two points. On the right, his own regiment broke, though there is no real indication as to whether it panicked or was physically swamped by sheer weight of numbers. Nor is it clear whether the fact that it had largely been recruited in the Highlands was a factor. At any rate, the 'Jacks' certainly seem to have had it in for them. Most of Claverhouse's regiments were massed in the centre, but as they came down the hill, Locheil's men, instead of joining with Glengarry in attacking the Earl of Leven's Regiment to their immediate front, veered off to their left in an attempt to join with Sleat and Sir Allan Maclean as they fell on Mackay's Regiment. It is unclear why they did so, but the likeliest explanation is that they preferred to go for the gap, rather than tackle Leven's men head on. Whatever the reason, this odd move had interesting consequences. In the first place it naturally exposed Locheil's men to terrible flanking fire from Leven's Regiment, and as a result no fewer than 120 of them were killed. By the time the wounded are added to the total, it is clear that the regiment must have been all but destroyed long before it reached the redcoat line and that only the physical impetus of the downhill rush kept the survivors going.

Seeing the Camerons shot down, Mackay decided to lead his two little troops of horse out through the substantial gap between Leven's and Kenmore's regiments, intending to finish them off. That he was able to contemplate, let alone execute a cavalry charge at this point, suggests that not all of the Highlanders were coming down

One of a number of Jacobite colours captured at Culloden and subsequently burnt in Edinburgh. Identification is surprisingly difficult., but the arms suggest it was most likely taken by Monro's 37th from John Roy Stuart's Regiment, or just possibly lost by Lord Kilmarnock's Footguards.

Opposite, while used by McIan to illustrate the Ogilvie tartan, this figure is actually an excellent copy of a portrait of James Drummond, Duke of Perth, a Lieutenant General in the Jacobite Army. Escaping from Culloden, he died on the ship carrying him to France.

Ruthven Barracks, near Kingussie, Badenoch. This military post was successfully held by Sergeant Terry Molloy and 12 men in 1745, but fell to the rebels in the following year. The Jacobite Army disbanded here after Culloden.

in a pell-mell rush, or that if they were, they had been halted by the heavy musketry. Whether or not this was the case, it was a disastrous move, for Claverhouse promptly counter-attacked at the head of his own cavalry and Belhaven's troop just as promptly turned and ran away from them. Worse still, in doing so, they contrived to ride over Kenmore's Regiment, throwing its ranks into confusion. Annandale's troop then followed suit, leaving Mackay, 'in the twinkling of an eye', alone but for his faithful servant. Disordered by their own cavalry and totally isolated in the middle of the battlefield, Kenmore's men were in no condition to resist as the feared clansmen came forward.

Evidently they were attacked by all three regiments in the Jacobite centre: Purcell's Irish (who oddly enough were criticised for charging like a herd of cattle), Clanranald's and Glengarry's, numbering 1,200 men in all, and outnumbering Kenmore's unhappy recruits by two to one. There is no evidence that they made any attempt to stand and, although the regiment's Lieutenant Colonel, John Fergusson of Craigdarroch was killed, family tradition asserts that he died simply because his servant had already made off with his horse. As for the men, only half of the regiment was afterwards rallied at Stirling, but to judge from Privy Council documents, most of the missing men were deserters rather than casualties.

Mackay's army was now cut in two, but what of his left wing? 'Balfour's Regiment,' said General Mackay, 'did not fire a shot and only half of Ramsay's made some little fire. Lieutenant Colonel Lauder was advantageously posted on the left of all, on a little hill wreathed with trees, but did as little as the rest of that wing, whether by his or his men's fault it is not well known.'

In fact, Mackay was being a touch ungenerous. An examination of the ground and the actual circumstances surrounding the collapse of these regiments suggests a different picture. While fighting was to continue for some time on the right, it is vital to appreciate that owing to the curvature of the hillside, the officers of Balfour's and Ramsay's regiments could see nothing but the Highlanders pouring down into the awful gap left by the rout of Kenmore's. It will have seemed to them that they were the only troops still standing and that accordingly it was time to withdraw. Their retreat was probably executed in good order at first, but when they reached the edge of the Urrard plateau and had to negotiate the steep, tree covered slope down to the road, it must have fallen apart. Sir John Maclean's men, outnumbered by three to one, are unlikely to have tried to close with Balfour's command earlier, but as soon as the redcoats fell into disorder, down they came while the Athollmen fell on Lauder's grenadiers in the birch wood. Initially, casualties were heavy, including Balfour himself, but while many officers and men fled back towards the Pass, George Ramsay managed to rally a substantial part of the brigade on the other side of the river. There, he not unnaturally, began to wonder what had happened to Mackay.

The general was, by his own account, having quite an adventurous time. Deserted by his cavalry, he momentarily found himself alone in

The back door of the barracks. A party of Highlanders tried to destroy the door with a barrel of combustibles, but were shot down from the loop-holes in the flanking tower. The fire was then doused by pouring water from the rampart above. Lacking artillery and scaling ladders the Highlanders then withdrew.

the middle of the battlefield, but looking around he saw what he rather quaintly described as a 'small heap of red coats' over to his right. Galloping across, he was agreeably surprised to find that half of Leven's Regiment had not only maintained its position, but provided a rallying point for the tougher elements of Mackay's and Kenmore's regiments. Better still, Mackay could see that Hastings' Regiment was also intact and marching up to join Leven.

Colonel Ferdinando Hastings was accounted venal and corrupt even by the lax standards of the age, but he was also a good soldier and when Mackay's Regiment was overrun, he refused his left flank, swinging it back in order to fire into the MacDonalds. Taking the hint, Sleat's men lost interest and immediately veered off in pursuit of the fugitives and ultimately the far more attractive prize represented by Mackay's baggage train. This prompt action not only saved Hastings' men, but allowed them to march across and join with the other survivors grouped around Urrard House. There, Mackay, untroubled by the Highlanders, for a time considered digging in, but then, with no word of Balfour's brigade, he retreated under cover of darkness, crossing the grisly battlefield and eventually linking up with George Ramsay on the far side of the River Garry.

At the time it must have seemed like a remarkable escape, but it came about partly through the chance killing of Claverhouse, which deprived the Jacobites of leadership at the critical moment, and partly as a consequence of what was to become a characteristic side effect of the Highland Charge. Killiecrankie is probably the first real instance of a full-blooded charge in action, but the same pattern was to be repeated time and time again right up to the final charge at Culloden. As we have seen, when the Highlanders came down the hill, the initial effect of the charge was very uneven. Mackay's line was penetrated at only two points. On the right, his

own regiment, which ironically enough numbered one of Locheil's sons amongst its officers, may simply have been swamped or at least intimidated by weight of numbers, while in the centre, Kenmore's unhappy recruits fled just as quickly, though they had at least the excuse that they were not only unsupported but had also been ridden over by their own cavalry. In both cases, the rout began *before* the Highlanders actually reached them and, ideally, the clansmen should then have taken advantage of the opportunity to roll up the exposed flanks of the adjacent units. Instead, not only did they go chasing straight through after the fugitives, but worse still, other units, including the unfortunate Camerons, simply followed after instead of pressing home their own attacks.

This may well have been a contributing factor in the disproportionately high casualties suffered by the officers of those units, which in turn increased the difficulty of maintaining any sort of control over them. By hanging back until Balfour's brigade fell into disorder amongst the trees, Sir John Maclean's Regiment and the Athollmen under Stewart of Ballechin came through pretty well unscathed. On the whole, the regiments which chased off Kenmore's men also seem to have avoided heavy losses, but Glengarry's Regiment was badly shot up as it ran past Leven's, for one of Glengarry's brothers, Donald Gorm, was slain at the head of his company— 100 stout fellows with a red stripe through their plaids—and another was wounded. Similarly, despite the partial collapse of Mackay's Regiment, Sir Allan Maclean lost a number of his officers, while Sleat was very roughly handled by Hastings, losing a number of his close relatives killed or wounded along with his second in command, a professional soldier named Sir George Barclay.

The precise circumstances in which these officers were killed or wounded is unknown,

Top, Colour belonging to the Chisholms captured at Culloden.
Bottom, Amongst the army's trophies was a 'blew silk colours with the Lovat arms, *Sine Sanguine Victor*'. As the motto is not Lovat's, the arms of Fraser of Inverallochie who commanded the battalion at Culloden are shown in this reconstruction.

Opposite, This fine study of a Cameron gentleman by McIan is interesting in depicting a Spanish *Escopeta*. Hundreds of these firelocks were landed by the Spaniards in 1719 and seen throughout the Highlands for many years afterwards.

but it is a truism that in an offensive casualties are minimised by closing with the enemy as quickly as possible. Therefore, it is undoubtedly significant that both the regiments to which these officers belonged, and the hard hit Camerons as well, were exposed to flanking fire as they moved across the front of the British line and tried to funnel into the gaps opened by the flight of Kenmore's and Mackay's regiments. It has been estimated that perhaps as many as a third of the Jacobite army became casualties and, by far the greater proportion of them, were probably shot down not in the final run up to the objective, but in avoiding coming to contact.

The all-important point is that when the Highland Charge worked, it did so through intimidation rather than the physical application of cold steel and Killiecrankie provides one of the clearest possible examples of this. The men who ran down the hillside towards Kenmore's and Mackay's were trading on the legacy of terror created by the awful massacre at Kilsyth, and afterwards it was stories of their own 'avalanche of steel' which in turn both heartened their successors and dismayed future adversaries. At the same time, it followed that if a regiment failed to be intimidated, the charge could end in bloody failure.

John Graham of Claverhouse had united the clans behind the old Lion Rampant banner of the Scottish kings, but with his death, the Jacobites lost their sense of direction. His successor, another regular soldier named Alexander Cannon, ordered the Highland army into a half-hearted and ultimately unsuccessful attempt to capture the little town of Dunkeld and thereafter the rebels were very much on the defensive until they were scattered by a cavalry brigade under Colonel Livingston in the following year, and then finally terrified into submission by the infamous (if a touch overblown) massacre in Glencoe. Nevertheless, Killiecrankie had well and truly established the notion that the clans might after all be a force to be reckoned with, and the next full scale Jacobite rising in 1715 saw a conscious effort on the part of the rebel leaders to exploit this fearsome reputation.

WERE YE AT THE SHERIFFMUIR?

The deep unpopularity of the enforced Union between the Scots and English parliaments in 1707 introduced a strong nationalist dimension to what might otherwise have remained a fairly pointless political and dynastic dispute. Consequently, when John Erskine, Earl of Mar (the less than charitably nicknamed 'Bobbing

After Prestonpans, almost all Jacobite soldiers had firelocks, but initially the story was very different and Woodhouselee noted 'rusty rapiers, matchlocks and fyerlocks and rag tag and bob taile' when the rebels first occupied Edinburgh.

A study, after the Penicuik artist, of a Highland sentry with firelock, bayonet and, unusually, a broadsword as well.

More Highlanders with firelocks and bayonets. Although the Jacobites are generally reckoned to have lost something in the region of 1,500 killed and wounded at Culloden, only 192 broadswords were recovered from the field.

Clansman with curved 'Turkish' blade. Woodhouselee observed that the front rank men were '1,400 of the most daring and best Militia in Europe', the rest being 1,000 'indifferent good' and 1,400 'good for nothing old men, shepherds and boys.'

John'), raised King James VIII's standard at Braemar on 6 September 1715, he attracted strong support from both sides of the Highland Line. Thus, when he finally lurched into action at Sheriffmuir, he had a numerically impressive force of some 900 cavalry, and while about half his 6,000-odd infantry were recruited from the same western clans (*ghillies* and all, this time, to judge by the numbers fielded) which had followed Claverhouse, the remainder were pretty evenly divided between the Athollmen and other Perthshire clans, northern levies under Seaforth, the Gordons, and about 900 men raised in the eastern Lowlands. Mar's army was much closer in character to the armies led by Montrose 70 years before than to Claverhouse's Highland host, but the way in which it was deployed on the frost-rimed heather shows that a fundamental shift in tactical doctrine had taken place.

At the outset of the Civil War, it was common to relegate Highland contingents to the second line and, other than in the chaotic shambles of Auldearn and Kilsyth, the great Montrose's tactical philosophy was to employ his regulars, be they Irish or Gordons, cavalry or infantry, first to soften up the opposition and secure his flanks, before letting the clansmen go forward to finish the business. Killiecrankie, however, had demonstrated that Highland swordsmen could be a potent force in their own right. So when Mar faced the Duke of Argyll on Sheriffmuir on Sunday 13 November, he, or more likely his professional chief of staff, General Hamilton, placed all the western clans in the front line, backing them up in the second line with the Lowlanders and, supposedly, less ferocious levies from the northern and eastern Highlands.

After some initial confusion while both sides groped around looking for each other, the 'Jacks' opened the battle with a Highland Charge. Unfortunately, the results fell rather short of their expectations and famously the left wings of *both*

armies ran away. The reasons for this mixture of success and failure are interesting and in large part arose from an unexplained blunder which sent most of the Jacobite cavalry to their right wing, leaving the left uncovered. Even without the assistance of these additional cavalrymen, it is likely that the rebel right wing would still have triumphed, for they appear to have caught Argyll's left while it was still deploying into line. Despite the Captain of Clanranald being shot off his rather too conspicuous white horse at the onset, the Highlanders surged forward in their usual terrifying fashion and, within four minutes, Glengarry had routed all but three of Argyll's regiments. Having done so, most of the clansmen happily spent the rest of the day chasing the fugitives towards Stirling, and as usual murdering those they caught. Behind them, however, it was all going wrong.

In the first place, Argyll still had three good regiments properly deployed and ready to meet the Jacobite left wing. Ordinarily, this might not have counted for much, but one of them, Shannon's (once Leven's) had seen off a Highland Charge at Killiecrankie. It is unlikely that many veterans of that fight were still standing in the ranks on Sheriffmuir, but while the clansmen were trading on the fearsome reputation of past massacres, Shannon's men were probably less likely than most to be to be intimidated by that reputation. As a result, the fighting on this wing was said be to 'indecisive', which probably means that just as the MacDonalds would do at Culloden 30 years later, the clansmen made a number of rushes or feints towards the regulars, breaking off each as soon as it became apparent they were not about to flinch. So long as they remained outside effective musket range, neither side was doing the other much harm, but the real decisive factor on this wing was Argyll's cavalry.

There were two squadrons of Portmore's 2nd Dragoons (the Scots Greys), two of Evans'

Mar Chuimhneachan air
Clann Donuill Ghlinne Comhann
a mhurtadh anns an oidhch 13
de an Fhaoilteach 1692 a rer
ordugh Righ Villiam III air
am beil cuimhne bheannaichte

4th Dragoons led by Lieutenant Colonel Henry Hawley and one of Stair's 6th Dragoons, all commanded by Colonel Cathcart of the Greys. Once it became clear that the Highlanders were not going to close, Argyll ordered him forward. Swinging wide, Cathcart came in on the Highlanders' flank and supposedly broke them, but as they only moved down the hill a short distance before rallying again, he is unlikely to have pressed his charge home. Instead, he contented himself with steadily forcing them back, probably thrusting or at least feinting forward with one regiment while the others covered. At any rate, his tactics were very successful and after three hours of continuous bickering, the Highlanders decided they had had enough and fled across Allan Water. Argyll, though well battered, was left in possession of the field and, although a substantial part of the rebel left wing was eventually marched against him, the light by that time was failing and he had taken advantage of the respite to dig himself in around a farm. Some of the 'Jacks' argued for one more attack to finish him off, but by this time the light was fading fast and so they withdrew back to Perth.

If one excepts the street battle in Preston on the same day, there was no fighting worth mentioning and less still during the abortive rising of 1719, but in 1745, King James's standard was raised for the last time at the head of what was to be widely known, not as the Jacobite army, but as 'The Highland Army.'

The gathering at Glenfinnan on 19 August 1745, like the one at Dalcomera more than 50 years before, was dominated by the western clans: the MacDonalds of Clanranald, Keppoch and Glengarry (although Sleat was a notable absentee), the Stewarts of Appin and the Camerons under Locheil. Other contingents came in as the rebels marched towards Edinburgh, but the westerners still made up

more than half of the army when it faced Sir John Cope at Prestonpans on 21 September 1745 and delivered what might almost be held up as a textbook example of a Highland Charge.

HEY JOHNNIE COPE

At first there was some doubt as to whether the Highlanders could deliver a charge at all, for on learning that Cope had disembarked his army at Dunbar, the Jacobites marched out to meet him and, after some preliminary manoeuvring, took up what appeared to be an ideal position on Falside Hill. There, they overlooked Cope's forces, drawn up on some flat ground near Prestonpans. On taking a closer look, however, the rebel commanders discovered to their dismay that a bog lay at the foot of the hill. As it would effectively stop any charge in its tracks and no one much fancied the idea of being casually shot down while vainly trying to struggle across it, they eventually decided to swing round to the right

Bankton House, Prestonpans, home of Colonel Gardiner of the 13th Dragoons, was called 'Olive Stob' in 1745. The final stages of the battle were fought around the house.

Opposite, a contemplative clansman in an unbleached woollen jacket, and rawhide pumps or *currans*.

under cover of darkness and attack Cope's position from the open eastern side.

Not surprisingly, the move went far from smoothly. A thick fog helped to screen their march, but as the rebels set off through the village of Tranent, every dog in the place set up a loud barking which alerted Cope and his officers to the fact that something was happening. Then, having cleared the village, the rebels followed a local volunteer along a little known path through the bog which he claimed to be a shortcut. Unfortunately, it also happened to be guarded by a picquet of dragoons who gave the alarm in good time for the general and his men to stand to their arms in readiness for the anticipated assault.

Sir John Cope, well described as a 'neat, fussy little man', had in fact spent the previous day shifting his regiments back and forth to counter every move or anticipated move made by the Jacobites, and now, far from being caught sleeping, he had them lined up and facing in more or less the right direction. Exclusive of officers, he had in total some 567 troopers serving in the 13th and 14th Dragoons, and 1,467 infantrymen of Murray's 57th and Lascelles' 58th, and a half battalion of Lee's 55th Foot. They were deployed in a single line, with the 14th Dragoons on the left and the 13th on the right, together with six small guns and two mixed detachments totalling about 200 infantry, earlier deployed as night picquets and the artillery guard.

Out in the mist, the rebels were getting flustered. The actual plan was straightforward enough. Once clear of the bog, the three MacDonald regiments, totalling some 850 men under the Duke of Perth, were immediately to march due northwards in order to leave sufficient room for the other front line 'division', or brigade, to deploy into line beside them. In the hurry, confusion and bad light, Perth – once unflatteringly dismissed as a 'silly horse racing boy'—went too far, so that when Lord George

Murray drew up his brigade, comprising 900 men of the Camerons, Appin Stewarts and Perth's Regiment, a large gap had opened up between the two. No attempt was made to close this gap, or fill it by bringing forward the Athollmen who were to form the reserve. Instead, both brigades rushed forward as soon as they formed.

In contrast to other battles under discussion, a number of intelligent eyewitnesses set down their often vivid impressions of what happened at Prestonpans, impressions which go far beyond simple statements regarding the movements of different units. John Home, one of the loyalist volunteers serving in Cope's army, heard rather than saw the clansmen coming forward: 'The ground between the two armies was an extensive corn field, plain and level without a bush or tree. Harvest was just got in, and the ground was covered with a thick stubble, which rustled under the feet of the Highlanders as they ran on, speaking and muttering in a manner that expressed and heightened their fierceness and rage. When they set out the mist was very thick; but before they had got half-way, the sun rose, dispelled the mist and showed the armies to each other.'

What it also showed was that, as a result of the initial hurry and confusion, the two widely separated Highland brigades were heading to the right and left wings of Cope's army, leaving his infantry in the centre completely uncovered except by the reserve trailing in the rear. Seeing half the Jacobite army storming towards them, the rather scratch collection of sea gunners and Invalids looking after Cope's six light curricle guns on the right, simply turned and ran off, while Captain John Cochrane's artillery guard, with considerably less excuse, 'gave a very irregular fire' and fell back into the ranks of the 13th Dragoons, who in turn also decided that discretion was the better part of valour at that point. Only Colonel Gardiner of the 13th showed

Equestrian portrait of John Gordon of Glenbuchat, after the Penicuik artist. This sketch corresponds with other eyewitness accounts describing him as bent with rheumatism and riding a grey Highland pony. Wearing a kilt on horseback is a touch eccentric.

French infantry equipment of the kind supplied to the Jacobites, along with firelocks and bayonets.

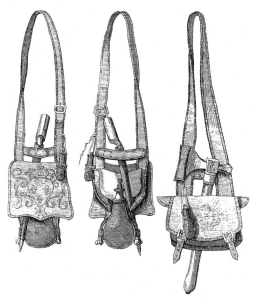

any fight and 'seeing the Officers who commanded the Foot, which his Regiment was appointed to guard, fall, the Colonel immediately quitted his Horse, snatch'd up a Half Pike, and took upon him the Command of the Foot, at whose head he fought, until he was brought down by three Wounds, one in his Shoulder with a Ball, another in his Forehead by a Broad Sword, and the third, which was a mortal Stroke, in the hinder Part of his Head, by a Lochaber Axe. This Wound was given him by a Highlander, who came behind him, when he was fetching a Stroke at an Officer, with whom he was engag'd.' Another, probably more reliable version, relates that his dismounting was actually the involuntary result of being shot and that the Highlanders promptly finished him off on the ground. Whatever the truth of the matter, he subsequently died on a mattress dragged out into the garden of his own home, Bankton House.

The British left wing collapsed equally quickly. Hamilton's 14th Dragoons made no attempt to charge the MacDonalds, but instead turned and made off after 'a few dropping shots' wounded both the commanding officer, Lieutenant Colonel William Wright, and his second in command, Major Richard Bowles.

On both wings, a fair number of Highlanders then behaved in the time-honoured manner by chasing straight after the fugitives, which meant that the greater part of Cope's infantry commanded by Colonel Lascelles were for a short time left standing in their original position while the rest of the battle passed them by. Much the same thing had happened at Killiecrankie, but without the heavy loss of officers suffered there, the Jacobite leaders were able to reassert a degree of control over their men. Lord George Murray, for example, was supervising the mopping up around Bankton House when he realised to his surprise that some bodies of regulars were still standing firm, and marched back to deal with

them. At what must have been the same time, according to Major John Severn's testimony to the subsequent court of inquiry: 'A large Body of their Left rush'd on obliquely on our Right Flank, and broke the Foot as it were by Platoons, with so rapid a Motion, that the whole Line was broken in a few Minutes.' With both flanks being rolled up at once, the whole lot with a few exceptions, followed the other fugitives back into the walled enclosures surrounding Bankton House. One of the exceptions was Colonel Francis Lascelles himself. Abandoned by his men, he was confronted by a party of Highlanders who relieved him of his sword and then rushed off again, so that in his own words he 'unexpectedly escaped [eastwards] to Seaton, between the Remainder of the left Column of the Rebels, and that next to it which were at a considerable distance from one another.'

By this time, it was all over bar the shouting and the Jacobites optimistically claimed to have disposed of no fewer than 500 of Cope's men, although the true figure would seem to have been nearer 150, with a further 368 wounded and 958 unwounded prisoners. By contrast, the rebels casually admitted to losing five officers and about 30 men killed, with a further 70 or 80 wounded. The disparity is easily explained by the fact that by

Bagot's Hussars. The Jacobite policy of clothing all their men in Highland dress even extended to cavalry units such as this rather raffish crew, in tartan jackets, plaids and reddish fur caps with white plumes.

A more dignified portrait of Glenbuchat, evidently 'improved' in Victorian times to provide a more romantic picture, though the features are still recognisable.

coming in on the flanks, rather than tackling the infantry in the centre head on, hardly anybody had the chance to shoot at them. Other than the 'very irregular fire' from the artillery guard and five rounds personally discharged by Colonel Whitefoord from the little curricle guns, they were pretty well untouched. It is significant, however, that four of the five officer casualties belonged to Murray's brigade, which received the contents of those guns.

Having broken the regulars, the clansmen as usual made the most of it. The greater part of the dragoons got away, but for the infantry there was to be no escape. According to one of the rebel cavalry officers, Lord Elcho: 'As soon as the pursuit began all the Principal Officers Mounted on horseback in order to Save and proteck Gen. Copes Officers as much as they Could, and had they not done it, Their would have been a great many of them kill'd, but as it happen'd their were very few.' The ordinary soldiers were not so lucky and the majority of the 150-odd dead were butchered in cold blood in the enclosures. Both the sudden victory and the striking disparity in casualties only served to inflate further the bloodthirsty reputation which was attaching to Highlanders. Cope's men had panicked, and that panic can in part be attributed to the fact that all three of his infantry regiments had been raised as recently as 1741. Not only had they never seen action, but although not formally designated as Scottish units, they had been very substantially recruited there—a good half of Cope's officers were certainly Scots—and it would be surprising if their familiarity with the Highlanders' legendary barbarity had not been a factor in the panic.

Jacobite leaders were well aware of the power of reputation and very deliberately traded on it. In the weeks which followed Prestonpans, the army doubled in size and French ships landed sufficient firelocks and bayonets not only to equip the new recruits, but also the half-armed mob of *ghillies*

noted by Woodhouselee. Comparatively few of the recruits were Highlanders: old John Gordon of Glenbuchat brought in a battalion from Strathavan, but they were armed with firelocks recovered from Prestonpans, and the greater number of the new levies came from the Lowlands. Lord Lewis Gordon, for example, brought in a battalion from the north-east which was temporarily added to the Duke of Perth's Regiment, Lord Ogilvy raised a battalion in Forfarshire and John Roy Stuart, a captain of grenadiers in the French *Royal Ecossois*, recruited what he optimistically entitled the 'Edinburgh Regiment'. Yet all of them, Highland and Lowland alike, were ordered to wear Highland clothing and to carry Highland weapons. Lord Ogilvy's officers, men from the east coast towns of Dundee, Arbroath and Montrose, were ordered to provide themselves with plaids, broadswords and targes, and to meet the demand, the latter were mass produced in Edinburgh. On one level, there is no doubt that this measure created a certain uniformity, which was no bad thing, but the primary purpose of kitting out Lowlanders as clansmen and referring to them all as the 'Highland Army' was to exploit the growing terror of Highlanders.

There is little doubt that they succeeded and a number of Jacobite memoirs contain droll stories of how English civilians were astonished to discover that they were not all bloodthirsty cannibals. They may in fact have succeeded too well, for while the celebrated march to Derby was undertaken in order to encourage either a French invasion or an English uprising, neither materialised. The decision to turn back at Derby has provided endless controversy for historians, but there was never any prospect of 4,000-odd men storming London. Although it was a political failure, this particular campaign was a remarkable military success, for the rebels went further south than might have been expected and got safely out

Opposite, examples of 18th century hairy sporrans do in fact exist, though they are generally smaller than the one depicted in this attractive study by McIan.

again without serious loss. The same could not be said of the battle of Falkirk, which although commonly accounted another famous Jacobite victory, actually bears a startling resemblance to the battle of Sheriffmuir 30 years before.

STORM ON FALKIRK MUIR

In January 1746, the rebels were besieging Stirling Castle when the British Army, led by Lieutenant General Henry Hawley, arrived at Falkirk on the 16th. In the circumstances, the Jacobites decided they had no alternative but to march out and fight him in the open and at 1pm in the afternoon on the 17th, a loyalist scout named Sprewell warned that they were making for the high ground of Falkirk Moor. A frantic race followed as both sides tried to gain the summit. 'We march'd to the Left', wrote Brigadier Cholmondley, 'near half a mile, but as we had hollow roads and very uneven Ground to pass, we were in great Confusion. Here we formed again, in my Opinion a very good Situation, but we were no sooner form'd but order'd a second time to take Ground to the Left, and as we march'd, all the way up hill, and Over very uneven Ground, our men were greatly blown.'

Hawley's men only just succeeded in reaching the top first, but the battle was a confused affair which began before the second line of either army had deployed properly. Naturally enough, the 'Jacks' had all their real Highlanders in the front line. From left to right were the Camerons (800), Stewarts of Appin (300), Frasers and Chisholms under the Master of Lovat (300), Lady Mackintosh's Regiment (200) led by MacGillivray of Dunmaglas, Farquharson of Balmoral's Deeside Battalion (150), Lord Cromartie's MacKenzies (200), Cluny's MacPhersons (300), and then the three MacDonald regiments under Clanranald, Glengarry and Keppoch, totalling no fewer than 1,550 men in four battalions. In close support, there were supposed to be three bodies covering the flanks and centre—the two Lowland battalions of Lord Lewis Gordon's Regiment (400), Lord Ogilvy's two battalion regiment (500), and the three battalions of the Atholl Brigade (600). Curiously enough, although the latter formation was recruited in Highland Perthshire, it was always accounted a Lowland regiment. Further to the rear, there was also a reserve comprising the rebel cavalry and a provisional battalion comprising five companies of French regulars.

Owing to the fact that both armies were hurrying towards each other from different angles, their respective positions were

Some very scruffy looking British regulars, as sketched by the Penicuik artist. Such illustrations of soldiers' actual appearance on campaign are very rare indeed.

HIGHLANDERS IN ACTION

misaligned, so that the right wing of each army overlapped the opposing left to a considerable extent. This was particularly marked on the south side of the moor where Hawley ordered his cavalry, some 800 troopers serving in Ligonier's (ex-Gardiner's) 13th, Cobham's 10th and Hamilton's 14th Dragoons, to move forward and secure the crest. In 1715, Hawley had successfully commanded Evans' 4th Dragoons at Sheriffmuir and as a result he had formed the opinion that Highlanders would not stand against cavalry. He had no hesitation, therefore, in ordering his cavalry to charge the MacDonalds at once, without waiting for infantry support. Unfortunately, both the circumstances and the result were very different. In the first place, in 1715, Cathcart and Hawley had been attacking or at least menacing the rebel clansmen in flank, rather than tackling them head on as Colonel Ligonier was about to do. Secondly, there had been a fundamental alteration in Highland equipment since that happy occasion. In 1715, only the gentlemen standing in the front rank had firelocks, those behind being equipped with Lochaber axes and other, more bucolic weapons. Even at Prestonpans, firelocks had been at a premium, but in the intervening period, all Jacobite soldiers were equipped with firelocks.

The result was perhaps only too predictable. The Highland front rank fired at long range as soon as the dragoons moved down off the crest and by all accounts did little damage. Instead of reloading, they then drew their swords and cocked their pistols which was doubtless vastly encouraging to the cavalrymen, but then, at the very last moment, the MacDonalds' second and third ranks fired a shattering volley at point blank range. A loyalist volunteer named William Corse afterwards averred that he 'saw daylight' appear in the dragoons' formation.

At this point, everything began happening at once. Cobham's and a handful of Ligonier's pressed on into the ranks of Glengarry's and Clanranald's regiments, '...throwing down every thing before them, and trampling the Highlanders under the feet of their horses. The most singular and extraordinary combat immediately followed. The Highlanders. stretched on the ground, thrust their dirks into the bellies of the horses. Some seized the riders by their clothes, dragged them down, and stabbed them with their dirks; several again, used their pistols; but few of them had sufficient space to handle their swords. MacDonald of Clanranald, chief of one of the clans of MacDonalds, assured me [James Johnstone] that whilst he was lying upon the ground, under a dead horse, which had fallen upon him, without the power of extricating himself, he saw a dismounted horseman struggling with a Highlander: fortunately for him the Highlander, being the strongest, threw his antagonist, and having killed him with his dirk, he came to his assistance, and drew him with difficulty from under the horse.'

Stirring stuff indeed, but savage though the fighting was, a three-deep line of men standing on foot is easily burst apart by cavalry and a number of Cobham's men broke through to attack the 1st Battalion of Lord Ogilvy's Regiment in the rebel second line. They were shy of firing into the MacDonalds' backs and a fair number of them, including one of the ensigns turned and ran for it instead. Had the other two Dragoon regiments been so resolute, the Jacobites might have been in serious trouble, but Hamilton's reprised their lamentable behaviour at Prestonpans by bolting straight back down the hill (and riding over the loyalist Glasgow Regiment), while the greater part of Ligonier's 13th and some of Cobham's made off to their right, passing across the rest of the rebel front line. As they rode by, they were roundly peppered by each regiment in turn, but elated by their success, the MacDonalds ignored Lord George Murray's pleas to stand fast and set off

Another left-handed Highlander, this time identified as Alexander MacDonald of Keppoch, killed at Culloden.

down the hill in pursuit. The other Highland regiments at once followed their example and, as they did so, a tremendous storm of wind and rain broke in all its fury, beating in the faces of the breathless British regulars. The storm was discouraging enough, but as the tempest was accompanied by a howling mob of clansmen flooding over the crest of the moor, it is perhaps hardly surprising that the majority of the regiments fled without firing a shot.

THE CURSED HOLLOW SQUARE

For a moment, the Jacobites were on the verge of a famous victory, but Barrell's 4th and Ligonier's 59th Foot, their front partly covered by a ravine, stood fast and fired into the flank of the Highlanders as they poured down the hillside. The result was dramatic. Colonel John Roy Stuart, who appears to have been commanding the rebel left, jumped to the conclusion that his men had fallen into an ambush and called on them to halt. He may have hoped to form a front against the redcoats, but his cry only added confusion to the panic. The Jacobite leaders were only too well aware of the Highlanders' propensity to scatter uncontrollably after delivering a charge and were no doubt hoping to employ the steadier Lowland units in the second line as a reserve against just such an occurrence. Unfortunately, as Colonel Sullivan complained, '...the cursed hollow square came up, took our left in flanc & obliged them to retire in disorder. There was no remedy nor succor to be given them. The second ligne, yt HRHs counted upon, went off, past the river & some of them even went to Bannocburn, & Sterling, where they gave out yt we lost the day.'

Thus, at the critical moment, just as at Sheriffmuir, the Jacobite left wing was in full retreat while the victorious right was scattered beyond recall. If anything, the situation was more serious, for the MacDonalds' charge had largely wasted itself on the fleeing Dragoons and hapless Loyalist Volunteers. Only three of the regular battalions on Hawley's left (Wolfe's 8th, Blakeney's 27th and Monro's 37th) suffered appreciable casualties, most of them officers abruptly abandoned by their men, and now the others began rallying behind the 'cursed hollow square'.

Encouraged by the rebels' confusion, Brigadier James Cholmondley succeeded in rallying Cobham's Dragoons and contemplated a local counter-attack with the 4th and 59th against some Highlanders whom he saw formed behind a barn and some cottages on top of the hill. Lord George Murray afterwards claimed that for want of a piper he had been unable to rally more than a handful of the scattered clansmen from the right wing, although the fact that the MacDonalds apparently could not stand the sight of him cannot have helped either. By some considerable exertion, he eventually pulled a couple of hundred men together, only to attract Cholmondley's unwelcome attention. Fortunately for him, the Brigadier was restrained by Major General Huske who also had three more battalions in hand (Howard's 3rd, Price's 14th and Fleming's 36th) and wanted to consolidate the position, while Brigadier Mordaunt rallied the rest of the regulars at the foot of the hill. Cholmondley argued that if they could be brought up at once, it would be possible to drive the Jacobites off the moor entirely, but by now darkness was falling and as Colonel Sullivan advanced towards them with French picquets (two companies of the *Ecossois Royal* and three Irish companies), Cholmondley's command fell back in good order towards the camp outside Falkirk.

The storm was at its height and although General Hawley had originally thought of holding both town and camp, his men were so battered and disorganised that he soon changed his mind and decided to pull back to Linlithgow instead. This decision came as a considerable relief to

Murray and Lord John Drummond—apparently the only Jacobite leaders apart from Sullivan still on the moor—and they gratefully threw their men into the town. After a little bickering in the streets, they evicted the rearguard, snapped up a few stragglers and then occupied Hawley's abandoned camp as well. This gave them sufficient excuse to claim a victory, but there was no real pursuit and no elation at their triumph.

At Prestonpans, a Highland Charge executed against Cope's raw Scots recruits had been spectacularly successful, both in itself and just as crucially in boosting the terrifying reputation on which any future successes would depend, but at Falkirk it attained neither objective. Despite being disrupted by Hawley's cavalry, the Highland Charge, in combination with the weather, had successfully chased off the loyalist units and most of the regulars. Any unit, however, which stood fast and refused to be intimidated was studiously ignored, and the better disciplined Lowlanders in the second line conspicuously failed to mop them up as intended. Consequently, the 'cursed hollow square' not only checked what should have been a merciless pursuit, but also provided a rallying point for those units which recovered from their initial panic. The Duke of Wellington was later to remark that all soldiers ran away from time to time, but the good ones came back again. Although General Hawley had been extremely despondent when he returned to Linlithgow, his men, once they had a chance to dry out, did not consider themselves to have been beaten. Most of them, unlike Cope's, were veterans of the war in the Low Countries and now confessed themselves ashamed of their behaviour and expressed a determination to do better next time. This did not bode well for the Highland Army.

When the British Army, now commanded by the Duke of Cumberland, moved forward again at the end of the month, the chiefs flatly refused to

1

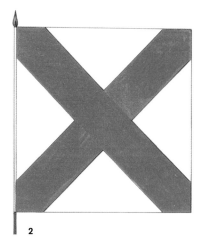

2

4

3

6

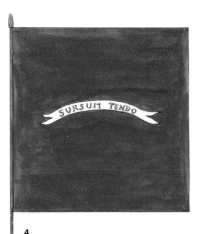

5

Above from left to right,
(1) Colour carried by Lord Ogilvy's Regiment, possibly by the 2nd Battalion. This was one of the few to be brought away from Culloden.
(2 & 3) Unidentified colours captured at Culloden. It is possible that they may have belonged to the Atholl Brigade.
(4) This colour was captured at Culloden. The motto is of the Kinloch family, which suggests that the colour may have been carried in the 2nd Battalion of Lord Ogilvy's Regiment, which was commanded by Sir James Kinloch.
(5) Unidentified colour captured at Culloden. A very similar one appears on the arms of Sir Alexander Bannerman of Elsick, and it may have been carried by his little regiment.
(6) Unidentified colour taken at Culloden. This one presents some difficulty as the motto belongs to the Sinclair family, none of whom raised any men for the Jacobites in 1745.

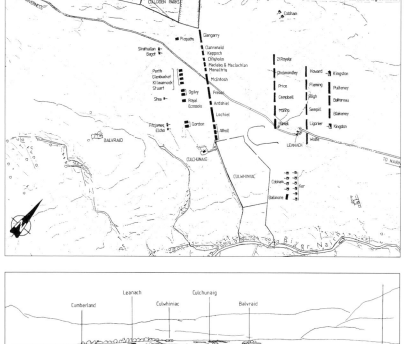

Top, this scale map shows the initial dispositions of both armies at Culloden. Some significant alterations were to take place before the shooting started.

Bottom, Panorama of Culloden, based on a well-known sketch by Thomas Sandby, a surveyor on the Duke of Cumberland's staff. The rebel second line is far too solid.

stand and fight a second time, and justified their stance with a remarkably perceptive analysis of what had gone wrong at Falkirk: '...the best of the Highland officers, whilst they remained at Falkirk after the battle, were absolutely convinced, that, except they could attack the enemy at a very considerable advantage, either by surprise or by some strong situation of ground, or a narrow pass, they could not expect any great success, especially if their numbers were no ways equal, and that a body of regular troops was absolutely necessary to support them, when they should at any time go in, sword in hand; for they were sensible, that without more leisure and time to discipline their own men, it would not be possible to make them keep their ranks, or rally soon enough upon any sudden emergency, so that any small number of the enemy, either keeping in a body when they were in confusion, or rallying, would deprive them of a victory, even after they had done their best.'

Falkirk had been Sheriffmuir all over again, but with the essential difference that in early 1716, the Jacobites were allowed to retreat northwards and disperse without fighting. This time, the British Army was determined to follow and finish them off once and for all. Only bad weather forced Cumberland into winter quarters at Aberdeen and allowed the rebels a respite, but while the Highland Army frittered away its time in minor operations, his own men prepared themselves both physically and mentally to face what would be the final Highland Charge.

According to newspaper reports, it was the officers of Barrell's Regiment who devised a new and improved bayonet drill calculated to demolish Highland swordsmen. The standard practice, based on 17th century pike drill, was to stand sideways on to the foe and level the bayonet-tipped firelock 'breast high' while grasping the butt end with the right hand. On the command 'Push!', the soldier would thrust it forward with the

Overleaf, Graham Turner's recreation of the battle of Culloden shows the Jacobite breakthrough on the extreme left wing of the British Army, just forward of the Leanach steading. The full force of the Highland charge was directed by accident or design against the 325 men of Barrell's 4th Foot, which after some particularly vicious fighting was overrun, temporarily losing one of its colours in the process. Two guns commanded by Sergeant Edward Bristo have also

been taken. Next to them, Monro's 37th Foot is still grimly hanging on, but its left flank is crumbling as casualties mount. Other Highland units are attempting to exploit this breakthrough by supporting the Camerons and Stewarts, largely unaware that the initial penetration is already being sealed off by four regiments brought up from the British second line by 'Daddy' Huske. Wolfe's 8th Foot are already in position and firing into the flank of

heel of his hand. It was very much a defensive rather than an offensive posture and now it was suggested that if the soldier was to alter his 'aim' and thrust to the right rather than straight ahead, he would strike at the Highlander's unprotected sword-arm rather than his targe. There was a rather obvious drawback to this cunning technique in that it entailed thrusting not at the clansman running directly towards the soldier, but at the next one along, while trusting at the same time that somebody else would take care of the immediate threat. The theory, supposedly based on classical precedent, also presupposed that the Highlanders would be so obliging as to offer themselves up to be slaughtered in this fashion and, despite glowing press reports, it is unlikely that the technique was successfully employed at Culloden. Nevertheless, there can be little doubt that the very devising and practice of the bayonet drill boosted the confidence of the soldiers and helped ensure that, instead of running, they would stand fast and employ a rather deadlier drill when the time came.

A MOOR NEAR CULLODEN HOUSE

The rebels' decision to stand and fight on Culloden Moor was a direct consequence of their failure to contest the crossing of the River Spey. Cumberland's sudden advance from his cantonments around Aberdeen in the second week of April 1746 took them by surprise. The 'Highland Division' and the Atholl Brigade were scattered across the hills, in Lochaber, Perthshire and in the far north, recruiting, besieging military posts and skirmishing with loyalist militia. Urgent orders were sent to recall them, but Cumberland successfully crossed the Spey on 12 April and when the rebel army drew up on Culloden Moor on the 15th, its concentration was still far from complete.

The choice of Culloden Moor as a battle-site by the Jacobite Quartermaster General, Colonel Sullivan, was loudly condemned at the time by Lord George Murray (and in just about every secondary source since), as being an open field which was at once unsuitable for Highlanders and at the same time offering every possible advantage to the British Army's artillery and cavalry. Yet this chorus of criticism defies both logic and precedent. At Prestonpans, the Jacobites had freely elected to fight on an even flatter stubble-covered cornfield against a British Army, which boasted a much higher ratio of artillery and cavalry than Cumberland's one, and, as Colonel Sullivan pointed out, Murray's own preferred site lay behind a ravine: 'I ask yu now yt knows the highlanders whither a field of Battle, where there is an impediment as yt Ravin was, wch is impractical for man or horse, was proper for highlanders whose way of fighting is to go directly sword in hand on the enemy?'

Far from being unsuitable, Culloden Moor was the best field for Highlanders between Inverness and Nairn, with an open slope to facilitate an unobstructed charge and boggy ground to cover both flanks. The pity of it is that circumstances would force the rebels to abandon Sullivan's chosen site in favour of another, less suitable one, a short distance away.

The Jacobites expected to face Cumberland at Culloden on 15 April, but now that he was actually in contact with their outposts, the Duke's advance had become more cautious and he halted that day in his cantonments around Nairn. The infantry were encamped at Balblair, just to the west of the town and the cavalry out at Auldearn, the scene of Montrose's victory a century before. Encouraged by this and the rather desperate hope that they might all be drunk in celebrating Cumberland's birthday, Lord George Murray proposed going on to the offensive with a dawn attack on the Balblair camp. Unfortunately, the plan miscarried. Too little time was allotted for reaching the start-line and when Murray very sensibly aborted the operation

the Atholl Brigade, while Ligonier's 59th, having temporarily divided in two wings to clear the steading itself (currently being used as a British field hospital) block it in front. Sempill's 25th are also in position and Bligh's 20th are hurrying up to the aid of Monro's.

Lord George Murray brought up the last uncommitted Jacobite reserves – the regular Royal Ecossois and Lord Kilmarnock's Footguards – in an attempt to widen the breach, but their intervention is too late. The Royal Ecossois will fire just one ripple of volleys and then retire in good order as the clans break.

The surviving Highland gentlemen in the front of the Jacobite formations have already discarded their firelocks – many indeed threw them away at the outset of the charge without bothering to fire them. Now, halted by Huske's counter-attack, they are unable to reply to the British crossfire, while the ordinary clansmen backing them up are also unable to shoot without blowing their leaders' heads off. By contrast, once Huske's men have finished moving into position, the British regiments surrounding them will soon muster no fewer than 1,900 rank and file, and while the front rank of each battalion stands fast with charged bayonets, the two ranks standing behind still number just over 1,200 men firing two rounds a minute at point blank range into a packed and virtually helpless target. Even if only 10% of these rounds take effect, the results are devastating and at least three regimental commanders, MacGillivray of Dunmaglas, Cameron of Locheil and Fraser of Inverallochy are down. Within a couple of minutes the Highlanders will break under the pressure. *Painting by Graham Turner*

well short of Balblair; he simply turned back with the leading brigade and failed to ensure that the message was passed back. As a result, one half of the rebel army was marching back to Culloden while the rest blithely kept on going and encountered Cumberland's picquet line before they realised what had happened.

The failure of the night march had two important consequences for the coming battle. In the first place, it exhausted the rebel soldiers to no purpose, and this in turn delayed the Highland Army's concentration on the intended battle position at Culloden before Cumberland arrived. As a result, the Jacobites had to fall back to another, much more hastily reconnoitred position a mile further to the west, and then the necessary redeployment was hampered by an almost total breakdown in relations between Lord George Murray and most of his colleagues. His habitual arrogance had won few friends in the past, but now his disastrous mishandling of the night march destroyed what little credit he had with the MacDonalds.

The fall-back position was an open stretch of common grazing land, on top of a narrow plateau, above Culloden House. On it, the rebels drew up in what appeared to be a secure position, with their right flank firmly anchored on the steading at Culchunaig and a drystone walled field falling down to the River Nairn known as the Culwhiniac Enclosure, while their left stretched across the rough grass to a similar wall surrounding the Culloden Parks. The ground over there was very boggy—James Johnstone, who fought as a volunteer in Glengarry's Regiment, remembered it was knee-deep in water in places—and initially most of the British cavalry was to draw up on the other flank by the farm at Old Leanach, simply because the ground there was firmer. As Cumberland advanced into contact, it became clear to him that his tactical options were very limited and there was no

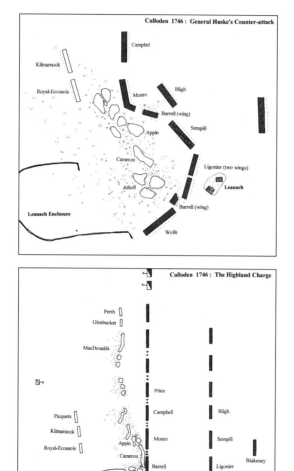

Top, **Key plan for Graham Turner's painting on pages 74-75.**

Bottom, **the dispositions of both armies have altered. Cumberland has extended his first and second lines towards his right, while the Jacobites have brought Perth's and Glenbuchat's regiments forward into the front line on their left. Only three battalions remain in reserve.**

obvious room for manoeuvre.

In the event, the cavalry led by Hawley and Lord Ancrum, and a half battalion of Highlanders belonging to the 64th and the Argyll Militia, broke through the Culwhiniac Enclosure walls and passed around the rebels' right flank, before climbing the slope again and stopping along the line of a shallow re-entrant south of Culchunaig. Here, they were faced by a hurriedly formed battle-line made up of four Lowland battalions and most of the rebel cavalry. Unable to see what was happening up on the moor, they prudently halted and waited there until the main engagement was decided.

With the outflanking move and most of Cumberland's cavalry thus checked, the main engagement turned into a remarkably straightforward contest between British regulars and Highland clansmen. On the right of the rebel army stood the three battalions of Lord George Murray's Atholl Brigade (500), then the Camerons under Locheil (600), the Stewarts of Appin under Ardsheal (150), one of Lovat's battalions commanded by Charles Fraser of Inverallochy (500), Lady Mackintosh's Regiment (500), Farquharson of Monaltrie's Deeside battalion, a small combined battalion of Macleans and Maclachlans (182), Chisholms (100), MacDonald of Keppoch's Regiment (200), MacDonald of Clanranald's Regiment (200), and the 1st Battalion of Glengarry's Regiment under McDonnell of Lochgarry (300). Initially, there ought to have been in the region of 3,380 Highlanders standing in the front line, but having taken up their position the rebels did not stay there for very long.

The turf-walled Leanach enclosure formed a salient, pushing out into the moor just forward of the British left wing. Shortly before the battle began, Lord George Murray decided to move his Atholl Brigade forward along the Culwhiniac wall in order to use it to mask his men from

Top, Culloden Moor today as viewed from Cumberland's front line. In 1746, it was largely covered with rough grass like this rather than heather, since it was used for common grazing.

Middle, partially reconstructed Culwhiniac Wall, with Culchunaig in the background. The exact line of the original wall was recently established by geophysical survey, confirming that Thomas Sandby mapped it pretty accurately in 1746.

Bottom, the reconstructed Leanach enclosure viewed from the northern corner of the Culwhiniac wall. The dark area of trees on the left horizon is where the rebels overran Barrell's Regiment, only to be caught in a deadly crossfire as General Huske counter-attacked.

Old Leanach cottage,
Culloden Moor. Recent
research has revealed that
the present building only
dates back to about 1760.
According to legend,
Jacobite wounded were
burnt alive in an adjacent
barn, but in fact the farm
appears to have been a
British Army field hospital.

Cumberland's guns, and, at the same time, formed them into battalion columns rather than line, in order to manoeuvre better around the obstacle when the Highland Charge was unleashed. He appears to have assumed that the rest of the front line would conform to this movement, but the MacDonald regiments over on the left flank refused to budge. They were in the first place annoyed that Murray had engineered the deployment of his own brigade on the right, but were also understandably unwilling to move out from the protection of the Culloden Park walls. Consequently, the whole line was not only thrown askew, but stretched as well so that great gaps opened up. It was then left to Colonel Sullivan to plug these gaps by bringing forward three more battalions from the second line. John Roy Stuart's Regiment was posted between the Appin men and the Frasers, while Perth's and Glenbucket's moved on to the extreme left. Despite this, the line still remained skewed and it appeared to the Duke of Cumberland and his officers that the intended axis of the rebel charge had shifted to their right, and so he in turn extended his front and second lines, in part by bringing forward the four troops of Kingston's 10th Horse from the reserve, and two troops of Cobham's 10th Dragoons who had earlier been scouting towards the north.

CLAYMORE!

At the outset of the battle, facing the Highlanders were seven battalions of infantry in the British front line, with 10 three-pounders, and six troops of horse, backed up by seven more battalions in the second line, and one more in reserve. The battle itself, or rather the shooting, appears to have started at about one o'clock in the afternoon, and oddly enough it was the rebel guns – 11 three-pounders – which fired first. A few minutes later, the British guns opened up in reply, but contrary to popular belief, there is ample

evidence that the bombardment lasted only a few minutes before the Highland Charge began. It was the first time the clansmen had been subjected to proper artillery fire and, instead of advancing steadily into musket range, they immediately set off at a run in order to minimise the time spent under fire. This had two unfortunate results. In the first place, the front rank men threw away their firelocks without making any attempt to fire a volley, and secondly, it was much more difficult for the Athollmen to manoeuvre around the Leanach Enclosure at speed. Of itself this was bad enough, but it also appears to have been compounded by a swerve to the right on the part of some of the units in the rebel centre. It has been suggested that they were trying to avoid the boggy ground north of the Inverness road, but whether this was the case or whether they were simply shying away from the hail of musketry which greeted them, the result was interesting. Firstly, however, it is necessary to look at what was happening on the rebel left.

The legend that the MacDonalds refused to charge because they had been denied the post of honour on the right is quite untrue. They were certainly unhappy about it and the story may have arisen from their failure to co-operate with Murray's earlier redeployment, but when the order was given to launch the charge, they started forward with everybody else. Conditions on this wing were very different to those on the right. They not only had further to go, but the boggy ground slowed them down to a walk rather than a headlong rush. This, in turn, meant that, unlike the clansmen on the right, they actually went through the normal preparatory stage of launching a charge.

They advanced slowly, fired their volley, and looked for signs of wavering in the regiments opposite. This time there were no such signs. As Cumberland himself reported: '...they came down three several Times within a Hundred Yards

Guidon captured from Gardiner's 13th Dragoons at Prestonpans and subsequently carried first by Lord Elcho's and then by Lord Balmerino's troop of the Prince's Lifeguards.

of our Men, firing their pistols and brandishing their Swords, but the Royals and Pulteneys hardly took their Firelocks from their shoulders...'. Had one of the British battalions lost their nerve, there can be no doubt that the MacDonalds would have come on, but after three attempts, and with a wary eye on the cavalry threatening the flank, they fell back and eventually fled the field, having suffered heavy casualties to no avail. This experience exactly paralleled that of the Jacobite left wing at Sheriffmuir.

On the right, by contrast, the charge was out of control. There was no attempt to intimidate the opposition, just a headlong rush forward which became all the more chaotic when Captain Godwin's gunners switched from firing ball to firing canister. The centre and right divisions collided by the Leanach Enclosure. Lacerated first by canister fire and then by two full battalion volleys delivered by Barrell's 4th and Monro's 37th Foot, they did not bother hanging about trying to intimidate anybody, but instead surged forward and overwhelmed Barrell's and the left wing of Monro's by weight of numbers. Both regiments suffered heavy casualties: Barrell's alone had 17 dead and 108 wounded out of 20 officers and 353 men present on the field, but they held on long enough for Brigadier Huske to organise a counter-attack with four battalions from the second line. One of them was Wolfe's 8th Foot, who are erroneously depicted in most secondary accounts standing at right angles to the British front line at the outset of the battle. In actual fact they only came forward now and with the three other battalions, Ligonier's 59th, Sempill's 25th (originally raised in 1689 as Leven's) and Bligh's 20th, wheeled in on the rebels and sealed off the penetration.

At this point, the Highlanders were jammed together in a mass, flayed by musketry on three sides. Captain Thomas Ashe Lee, an officer in Wolfe's, related how his regiment 'marched up to the enemy, and our left, outflanking them, wheeled in upon them; the whole then gave 5 or 6 fires with vast execution, while their front had nothing left to oppose us, but their pistolls and broadswords; and fire from their center and rear, [as, by this time they were 20 or 30 deep] was vastly more fatal to themselves, than us.' Another, unnamed officer in the regiment, wrote that they 'plied them with continual fire from our rear and fixt bayonets in front'. Exactly the same thing was described rather more explicitly by a Corporal in Monro's, who stated that 'the Front Rank charged their Bayonets Breast high, and the Center and Rear Ranks kept a continual Firing...'. Protected by a hedge of bayonets and firing at point-blank range, the four regiments may have killed or wounded as many as 700 clansmen in just two terrible minutes, and it is no coincidence that the macabre outline of that doomed column can be traced in the mass graves still to be seen on the moor.

Unsurprisingly, the clansmen broke. They had thrown everything into the penetration rather than trying to press home frontal attacks all along the line. At another time, they might have widened the breach, rolling up the rest of the front line as they did at Prestonpans and Falkirk, but at Culloden they became jammed together in a death-trap. Lord George Murray brought up the *Ecossois Royal* and Lord Kilmarnock's shabby Footguards in an effort to relieve the pressure, but it was too late. The *Ecossois Royal* fired a volley for the sake of honour and then got themselves ambushed by the loyalist Highlanders under Captain Colin Campbell of Ballimore as they retreated along the Culwhiniac wall.

This was the signal for Hawley's cavalry to push across the re-entrant south of Culchunaig and climb up on to the moor. The move was facilitated by the prudent withdrawal of the four Lowland battalions who until now had been holding the crest, and once on top they found

William Boyd, Earl of Kilmarnock and a Colonel in the Jacobite army at Culloden.

little to stop them. Kilmarnock's Footguards promptly dissolved into a rabble of fugitives and although the *Ecossois Royal* made a fight of it, one wing or battalion of the regiment was quickly surrounded and forced to surrender. At pretty much the same time, Cumberland himself galloped up to the squadron of Cobham's on his right and ordered them forward with a cry of 'One more brush my lads for Old Cobham!' They too encountered little resistance beyond a volley from the Irish Picquets and then had the satisfaction of meeting with Hawley's troopers in the middle of what had been the rebel position. Reunited, all three cavalry regiments completed the victory with a textbook pursuit down the Inverness road. In little more than an hour, it was all over and while there is no doubt that the pursuit was murderously ruthless, it was no worse than those conducted by the Highlanders themselves after their own great victories at Kilsyth and Prestonpans.

Bayonet drill 1746, as demonstrated by a Corporal of the recreated Pulteney's 13th Foot.

HIGHLAND REGIMENTS

Opposite, this print by McIan is closely based on a near contemporary engraving by Van Gucht of a Highland officer, presumably belonging to the 42nd c.1759, as evidenced by the blue facings, gold lace and the red overstripe on the tartan.

Although Culloden was described by one of its victorious participants as 'the bloodiest battle in the memory of man', it neither destroyed the clan system, nor led directly or even indirectly to the infamous Highland Clearances. The battle and the counter-insurgency operations in the hills which followed destroyed the threat of another Jacobite rising, but that was hardly the same thing, for not since the forfeiture of the Lordship of the Isles had a substantial part of the Highlands been united as an autonomous power bloc. It is a striking fact that although Highlanders and Jacobitism are now virtually synonymous in the popular imagination, more of them turned out to fight for King George in 1745 than were persuaded to follow the Pretender's banner. In real terms, only the pro-Jacobite clans of the Great Glen and Lochaber were involved in the Rising, and it was they, rather than the Highland peoples at large, who directly suffered as a result of its failure.

The substantial changes in Highland society in the 18th century actually came about not through dramatic military action, but through the ending of their largely self-imposed isolation from the rest of the country. That, in turn, was the direct result of General Wade's road building. Primarily intended to facilitate the rapid movement of troops to any trouble spots, the roads also opened up the Highlands commercially and culturally and, without a shot being fired, encompassed the eventual disintegration of the clans. While the reintegration of the Highlands into the mainstream of the new British state was arguably well underway before the Rising, it was accelerated afterwards by the close-knit involvement of a surprising number of Highland families with the British Army.

The case of the MacBeans provides a notable example of how families not only came to be identified with the army, but intermarried with other army families to create what was in effect a military caste transcending the old clan loyalties. In the 1880s, Colonel Forbes MacBean left this memoir:

'My great-great-grandfather was minister of the High Church [Presbyterian] at Inverness for upwards of forty years. One of his sons [Forbes] was a maj.gen. of R.A.; two of his sons were – one [Frederick] col.-comg. 6th Foot, the other maj. of the 14th and 71st Regts. The eldest had six sons, all in the army, viz; Sir William KCB and KTS gen. and col.-in-chf. 92nd Highlanders; Frederick, KH, col. 84th Regt.; Forbes, col. R.A.; Archibald, Lt.-gen. R.A.; Alfred, capt 93rd Highlanders; Alexander, lt. 83rd Regt. The last two died young.'

Of itself, this recital might seem a formidable enough record of attachment to the British Army, but the Reverend Alexander MacBean also fostered the orphan children of another Highland minister, Archibald Bannatyne from Dores, on the shore of Loch Ness and two of them were to follow military careers. Robert Bannatyne joined the East India Company's service and was killed at Conjeveram in 1758, while his younger brother William was Adjutant of the 13th Foot and a sister, Ann, married a son of Grant of Sheuglie, Major Gregor Grant of the 58th Foot.

It is important to note that few of this particular extended family actually served in Highland regiments, and once again, there was nothing at all unusual in this. The Highlands had long been a fertile recruiting ground for the regular army, as well as a few foreign ones, and for some reason the Royal Scots in particular, although generally accounted a Lowland regiment, drew a great many of both its officers and men from the hills throughout the 18th century. It is perhaps appropriate that an illegitimate daughter of William Bannatyne was to marry the son of one of the original members of the Black Watch.

This famous regiment was by no means the first regular Highland unit—Argyll's, Grant's and Strathnavar's had all been raised and disbanded during King William's War in the 1690s—but the Watch was different, in that unlike its predecessors, it was clothed and equipped in the Highland

manner, with belted plaid and broadsword, as well as firelock and bayonet. This was because it had its origin in the Highland Independent Companies, a para military police force or *gendarmerie* set up on the recommendation of General Wade in 1724. There had been similar companies raised before and disbanded again when it was realised that on the whole they contributed to rather than diminished the crime rate.

As Wade complained: 'For want of being put under proper regulations, corruptions were introduced, and some who commanded them instead of bringing criminals to justice (as I am informed) often compounded for the theft, and for a sum of money set them at liberty. They are said also to have defrauded the government by keeping not half their number in constant pay.'

Wade's companies were probably no better, for like their predecessors they had to be entrusted to the command or rather proprietorship of local gentlemen and there was an obvious temptation

for those gentlemen to regard them first and foremost as a convenient source of income, both for themselves and for their needy friends and dependants. Membership of the early Watch was, in that wonderfully evocative 18th century expression, a 'job' and the maintenance of law and order was very much a secondary consideration.

GENTLEMEN AND MUTINEERS

The earliest historian of the Highland regiments, David Stewart of Garth, pompously asserted that: 'Many of the men who composed these companies were of a higher station in society than that from which soldiers in general are raised; cadets of gentlemen's families, sons of gentlemen farmers, and *tacksmen*, either immediately or distantly descended from gentlemen's families;- men who felt themselves responsible for their conduct to high-minded and honourable families, as well as to a country for which they cherished a devoted affection.

'Hence it became an object of ambition with all the young men of spirit to be admitted, even as privates, into a service which procured them the privilege of wearing arms. This accounts for the great number of men of respectable families who were to be found in the ranks of the Black Watch...'.

There was a considerable measure of truth in these claims. Men such as Malcolm MacPherson, the son of the *tacksman* of Drimminard and Alexander Grant, referred to by Lovat in 1737 as a 'soldier in Captain Grant's company, and son to Robert Grant in Milntown, a cousin-german of Sheuglie's', were typical of those who joined the Watch. It was all very cosy and it was Grant's son, William, who married William Bannatyne's daughter, while another son, Charles, became a director of the East India Company. It is perhaps equally significant that Grant, known as 'Alexander the Swordsman', served in Glengarry's rebel regiment during the '45 and that Malcolm MacPherson was to be shot for his part in the

Black Watch grenadier cap c.1739. This is the original pattern embroidered mitre cap worn by grenadier company officers of the 43rd before the adoption of the more familiar fur cap at some time in the 1740s.

infamous Black Watch mutiny of 1743.

Not unnaturally, the government was less than impressed by the set-up. It wanted an efficient constabulary, not a species of gentleman's club maintained at public expense, and in an effort to exert some proper control over the companies, they were formally embodied as the 43rd Regiment of Foot on 25 October 1739. It would be no exaggeration to say that this alteration in their status came as a salutary shock to the Highland gentlemen in the ranks, particularly since four more companies were authorised, to be recruited by beat of drum just like every other regiment in King George's army. They immediately looked down on the newcomers, disdainfully referring to them as 'scrubs', but the imposition of military discipline and a proper regime of training was equally unwelcome. Stewart of Garth relates that, 'when this regiment was first embodied, it was no uncommon thing to see private soldiers riding to the exercising ground followed by servants carrying their firelocks and uniforms.' Such men did not take easily to the long hours of hard work needed to perfect their 'evolutions' and master the arcane art of 'platooning', and the only surprise is that they should have waited for so long before taking what was in effect industrial action.

The catalyst came in 1743, when the 43rd was quite casually earmarked for service in the escalating war on the Continent. There was nothing in the least sinister about this and had the 43rd been a regularly enlisted regiment of the line there would have been no problem. A substantial number of the Watch had joined up merely for the privilege of swaggering around carrying the arms denied to lesser mortals by the 1724 Disarming Act and the thought that they might actually be called upon to use them in foreign adventures was not part of the plan. Led by Corporal Malcolm MacPherson and his cousin Samuel, they decided to desert.

What followed constituted a mutiny only inasmuch as it was a collective effort, rather than

Piper Donald MacDonald, print published by Bowles in 1743, depicting one of the Black Watch mutineers. Coloured versions of this print show the pipe banner to be yellow (or yellow buff) with a red cross–the old Independent Companies' badge.

a series of individual attempts to head for the hills. About 120 men were involved and, in the end, only three of them, the two MacPherson cousins and Farquhar Shaw, an ex-drover who had resisted arrest, were shot, while the remainder of the would-be deserters were drafted into regiments serving in the Mediterranean garrisons, the West Indies and Georgia. Apart from some untoward excitement at the time, the rest of the regiment gave no real cause for concern and behaved with appropriate gallantry at Fontenoy in 1745, though whether they really executed a Highland Charge there is perhaps open to question. With the European war well underway, a further three 'Additional' or depot companies were formed in order to process new recruits (most regular battalions had to make do with a single 'Additional' company) and a second regiment, the Earl of Loudoun's 64th Highlanders, was authorised in 1745. The Jacobite rising that summer found the regiment still in the process of being formed with its embryonic companies scattered the length and breadth of the Highlands. While some of them gave good service, stiffening the Independent Companies and fighting at Culloden, a number of men defected to the rebels under at least two of the regiment's officers, McDonnell of Lochgarry and MacPherson of Cluny.

The problem, as with the earlier trouble with the Watch, lay in the way in which they were recruited. Ordinary regiments of the line relied upon sending out small parties of officers and NCOs to find more or less willing individual volunteers at markets and 'feeing marts' or hiring fairs. It was a slow and tedious business, characterised by a later agent as 'horrid drudgery', but Highland recruiters sought to find their men by exercising their often considerable local influence and milking old clan loyalties.

It was no coincidence that men such as Lovat were appointed to command companies. As the chief of Clan Fraser, he had little difficulty in finding enough men, whether from amongst his own

people or from 'friends' willing to oblige him. Even when he was deprived of his company on the embodiment of the 43rd, he was still able to call upon neighbours such as Glengarry for a few recruits to bring it up to its authorised strength and so conceal the extent to which he had been pocketing the pay of non-existent soldiers.

In the early days it was comparatively easy to find such men, for it was still widely accepted that a chief had the right to call them out. As late as 1778, Hugh Mackay of Bighouse was still able to write: 'The people of this country are so much attached to their masters that with them they do not scruple going to any distant country. But I was afraid should I send a part of the men and I do not go with them... they would take in their heads they would be sent to other regiments, and not to your Grace's [the Duke of Gordon's Northern Fencibles]; which would occasion a great stagnation in my recruiting.'

The other downside was that if they were so attached, they might consider themselves to be

The same recreated officer viewed from the rear provides a good picture of the old belted plaid. Like most infantry officers serving in North America, he carries a lightweight fusil as his primary weapon.

Opposite, front view of a recreated Black Watch officer, c1760, wearing an unlaced 'frock' or service jacket and a white or very pale buff waistcoat, as seen in a portrait of Captain John Campbell of Melfort.

serving their 'master' rather than the King, and should an officer such as McDonnell of Lochgarry decide to switch sides and declare for the Pretender, they would dutifully follow him. The authorities were far from satisfied with this state of affairs. At the end of the European war, the Black Watch, renumbered as the 42nd Foot, retained its Highland designation, clothing and weapons, but there was considerable opposition to their being re-deployed in the hills, as a Scots peer, Lord Findlater made clear to the Duke of Newcastle: 'It is said that ther is an intention to turn the two Highland Regiments into Independent Companies to be sent to the Highlands... I am sure it wou'd prove a most pernicious scheme, for it wou'd effectively spread and keep up the warlike spirit there and frustrate all measures for rooting it out.'

Given the attraction which the old Watch held for swaggering young men, eager to walk abroad armed to the teeth in defiance of the 1724 Disarming Act, Findlater was probably right. At any rate, the 42nd was posted to Ireland where it would remain, foreign adventures aside, for the rest of the century.

RENEGADES AND REDEMPTION
The customary Treasury-led retrenchment which followed the Peace of Aix-la-Chapelle in 1748 saw the Army's infantry reduced to three regiments of Footguards and just 48 numbered regiments of the line. Consequently, the subsequent resumption of hostilities against France in 1756 saw an equally customary scramble to raise fresh regiments. Following the earlier desire to 'root out the warlike spirit', which had seen another and yet more draconian disarming act, and the Heritable Jurisdictions Act of 1747, which deprived the chiefs of their still considerable feudal powers, the government tentatively embarked on the experiment of raising two fresh Highland battalions. Initially designated as the 62nd and 63rd Highlanders, no sooner were they authorised than

they were taken out of the line and briefly retitled the 1st and 2nd Highland battalions respectively, before coming back into the line again as the 77th and 78th Highlanders. At first sight, it is not clear why this curious sequence of events came about, but the resultant drop in official seniority doomed both regiments to disbandment at the end of the war. This may well have been down to a certain uneasiness on the part of the authorities as to the activities of one of the commanding officers, Lieutenant Colonel Commandant Simon Fraser, the one-time Master of Lovat.

There was certainly nothing about the other commanding officer, the Hon. Archibald Montgomerie, which might have given rise to any concern. A Lowlander and scion of a prominent Ayrshire family with impeccably Whig credentials, he proceeded to raise his 77th Highlanders in the normal way by sending out recruiting parties all over Scotland. When the completed battalion was inspected at Nairn on 9 March 1757, it was noted that his own company had been recruited in Atholl and Strathdearn, that Major James Grant's came from Strathspey and that Major Alexander Campbell had been picking up recruits from the length and breadth of the western Highlands. As for the rest, one company was raised on the island of Skye and others came from the northern counties, from Aberdeenshire, Perthshire, Edinburgh and Glasgow. While a fair number of the recruits picked up in the two cities were no doubt Highlanders, the regiment was by no stretch of the imagination a clan levy in the old style. The same could not be s aid of Simon Fraser's battalion.

Fraser in fact had an extremely chequered, if not to say unsavoury history. In 1745, he was attending St. Andrews University when his poisonous old father, Lord Lovat, insisted that he lead the clan regiment in the Pretender's service. Like many others, Fraser claimed to have done so with considerable reluctance, but in his case adherence to the doomed Stuart cause was at best lukewarm

The 'hard and rapacious' Major General Simon Fraser (1726-1782). Although the uniform is evidently of a later period, the marked resemblance to his father, Lord Lovat, is quite unmistakable.

Opposite, **An excellent print after Van Gucht from Grose's *Military Antiquities*, providing one of the clearer 18th century illustrations of the belted plaid. Note how the corporal, on the right, has his hair brushed up under his bonnet.**

and may have been downright treacherous. There is some reason to believe that he and his regiment were amongst those who ran away at Falkirk and at Culloden, and he managed to avoid appearing on the field at all. There was one Fraser battalion on the moor, led oddly enough by a Lowlander from Aberdeenshire, Charles Fraser of Inverallochy, but Simon Fraser's own battalion was still marching up the road from Inverness when the first fugitives from the debacle began pouring down it.

According to tradition, he promptly faced his battalion about and marched it straight back to Inverness, still with pipes playing and colours flying. Tradition, however, is much less clear as to what happened next. There might well be an innocent explanation for his tardy arrival at Culloden and there is a story that, having safely returned to Inverness, he loudly proposed to barricade and hold the bridge over the River Ness, but was scornfully dissuaded by some local worthies. The obvious assumption is that Fraser was proposing to block it against Cumberland's men, but another Jacobite fugitive, James Johnstone, recalled hearing a s hort but intense burst of fire as he made a detour around the town. None of the many contemporary letters by Cumberland's officers make mention of any resistance in the town, which raises an interesting question as to what was really going on. Another local tradition relates that a party of the loyalist Argyll Militia had infiltrated the town and unsuccessfully attempted to close the bridge against the retreating Jacobites. There is no evidence to support this inherently unlikely tale, but Simon was very much his slippery father's son, and there is perhaps every reason to suspect that he changed sides on the afternoon of 16 April 1746 and did indeed attempt to hold the bridge, not against King George's forces, but against his own colleagues in the Jacobite army!

Such a hypothesis would account for his subsequent swift and miraculous rehabilitation in the eyes of the government. In due course, his

father was captured, given a fair trial and executed. Young Simon voluntarily surrendered in August 1746, after a delay which suggests that he may have been waiting for certain guarantees before coming in. Although duly condemned for high treason, he was obliging enough to use his influence on behalf of the government in a contested by-election by persuading his uncle, the Laird of Grant, to stand down in favour of its preferred candidate. This timely and public-spirited act won him conditional release from Edinburgh Castle to study law at Glasgow University and then a full pardon in 1750. By now, he had obtained the patronage of the Duke of Argyll and finally distanced himself from any taint of Jacobitism by serving as a prosecuting counsel in the infamous Appin murder trial of 1753. It was all very cosy and it was Argyll who was instrumental in obtaining for him the necessary Letters of Service to raise what would become the 78th Highlanders.

The composition of this regiment, soon to become famous for its part in the taking of Quebec, was quite startling. Many of them were his own clansmen, such as Simon Fraser of Inverallochy, the son of the man who had died commanding the Frasers at Culloden, but others also included John Macpherson, a brother of Cluny, John MacDonell of Lochgarry, Alexander Cameron of Dungallon,

Ronald Macdonald of Keppoch, a brother of MacDonald of Boisdale and a son of Barisdale, and Charles Stewart, son of the dashing Colonel John Roy Stuart, the Jacobite officer who was the real model for Robert Louis Stevenson's Allan Breck.

Despite the token presence of men such as John Campbell of Ballimore, who was the son of a loyalist officer killed at Culloden, the 78th was to all intents and purposes a 'turned' Jacobite unit, which may be why contemporary paintings show a brown tartan being worn, instead of the usual Government sett. The authorities were in no doubt about its odd status and Viscount Barrington, the Secretary at War, not only pushed both Highland regiments further down the line of seniority, but wrote very firmly that: 'I have no doubt that the additional Highland Companies will be sent to America as soon as they are raised; and that none will be suffered to remain in the Country on any pretence.' Given the fact that a French invasion remained an uncomfortable possibility right up until Admiral Hawke's magnificent victory in Quiberon Bay two years later, this cautious attitude was understandable.

Over the next few years, a handful of other Highland battalions were raised and just as promptly shipped abroad. The 42nd, now calling themselves 'The Old Highland Regiment', temporarily gained a second battalion along with Royal status. Another Lowlander, Major Robert Murray Keith, who had served with the Scots Brigade in Holland, raised the 87th Highlanders, which together with John Campbell of Dunoon's 88th, served in Germany (effectively as one two-battalion regiment) and an American professional soldier named Staats Long Morris took the 89th Highlanders to India. After the ending of the French invasion threat, the government was able to take a slightly more relaxed attitude to its Highland units. A number of Independent Companies was authorised for recruiting purposes and some were combined to form Campbell's 100th which served in the Channel Islands and Martinique, and

Johnstone's 101st, which remained in Scotland as a depot battalion for the 87th/88th. Shortly before the war ended, two more regiments received letters of service: William Gordon of Fyvie's two-battalion 105th which served in Ireland, and Allan Maclean's 116th, earmarked for America, but still incomplete when peace was signed.

Although all of them, except 1/42nd, were disbanded then, or shortly afterwards, the great statesman, William Pitt the Elder, famously boasted: 'I sought for merit wherever it was to be found, it is my boast that I was the first minister who looked for it and found it in the mountains of the north. I called it forth and drew into your service a hardy and intrepid race of men, who when left by your jealousy became a prey to the artifice of your enemies, and had gone nigh to have overturned the State in the war before the last. These men in the last war were brought to combat on your side; they served with fidelity as they fought with valour and conquered for you in every part of the world.'

Pitt was an enthusiastic supporter of the new Highland regiments, though Simon Fraser's patron, the Duke of Argyll, has a far better claim to be their only begetter. In reality, the Government had approached the question of the Highland regiments with considerable circumspection. Not only were they shipped abroad with indecent haste and then disbanded at the war's conclusion, but with the exception of Fraser, the letters of service had been bestowed not upon clan chiefs but on professional soldiers, Lowlanders for the most part, picked for their reliability rather than their supposed ability to pull large numbers of clansmen out on to the heather.

This can be seen clearly in the case of the 89th Highlanders. Although he himself was an American, Staats Long Morris had contracted a fortunate marriage with the Dowager Duchess of Gordon, and the regiment has consequently been claimed as a precursor of the more famous 92nd (Gordon) Highlanders. Unlike Fraser's 78th, there was a

A surprising number of Highlanders served in the Royal Artillery. Captain Godwin's company at Culloden included a Simon Fraser and a Charles Grant, but the most notable was Forbes MacBean, who joined in 1743 and died a Lieutenant General.

notable absence of clansmen in the ranks. What was more, apart from the young Duke himself, a captain, but forbidden by the King from going abroad, only six of the regiment's subalterns bore the name of Gordon, and two of them were the Duke's infant brothers. While the other officers did include a brother of the MacGillivray of Dunmaglas killed at Culloden leading Lady Mackintosh's Regiment, the majority of the 89th's officers were Lowlanders from Aberdeenshire and Banffshire. This was reflected in the rank and file whom they recruited and, although the original muster rolls have not survived, all the deserter descriptions relate to men born and bred in Aberdeen and other Lowland parishes throughout the north-east of Scotland.

THE FIERY CROSS LIT ONCE AGAIN

It is hard to escape the impression that the 89th's Highland designation was merely a compliment to Morris's high-born lady and, while there is no doubting the influence that she and others were able to exercise in obtaining recruits, there was in reality no difference between most of the new so-called Highland units and other Scottish regiments such as the 70th (Glasgow) Regiment, apart from the fact that the former generally wore kilts. It is just as difficult to escape the impression, at this stage, that neither the government nor the chiefs themselves were contemplating the reappearance of old-fashioned clan levies. The Rising was still too recent a memory for anyone in authority to countenance what might be regarded as private

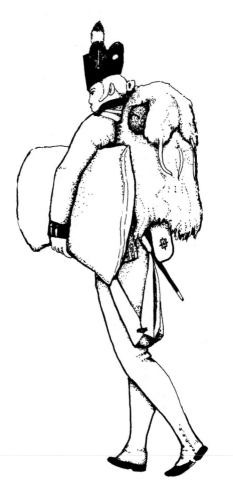

Private, 1/Royal early 1790s, after Beechey. So strong were the regiment's Highland links that, as late as the early 1800s, an unsuccessful request was made for it to adopt Highland dress.

Officer, 1/Royal, after Beechey, early 1790s. Despite the lure of the kilted regiments, many Highland gentlemen such as MacDonald of Kinlochmoidart still chose to join the Royal Scots.

armies, while the chiefs, although keen to make their way in the world, were still acting with equally understandable circumspection.

The catalyst was Simon Fraser's corps of renegade Jacobites. Their successful probation, which included fighting with some distinction in the glorious victory at Quebec, opened the way for an extraordinary, but ultimately doomed, last flowering of the old clan system. Where the promoters and recruiters of Highland regiments had proceeded with a degree of caution during the Seven Years War, the outbreak of the American War of Independence in 1775 saw an enthusiastic rush on all sides to raise what were not merely Highland regiments, but *clan* regiments!

Predictably enough, Simon Fraser, now elevated to the rank of Major General, was the first off the mark with two battalions of his new 71st Highlanders, but the others followed thick and fast. Lord McLeod raised two battalions of the 73rd in the Highlands, though Campbell's 74th was raised half in Argyllshire and half in Glasgow and the Lowlands. Lord MacDonald similarly recruited most of his 76th in the western Highlands, but two companies had to come from the Lowlands and a third from Ireland. Murray's 77th came from Atholl and Seaforth's 78th from the north, while William Gordon of Fyvie, who had raised the 105th in the last war, now recruited his 81st in and around Aberdeen. In all, 10 nominally Highland battalions (including a new 2nd Battalion for the Black Watch) were brought into existence for general service and three more Highland fencible battalions were levied for home service. Once again, all but two of the battalions, which happened to be serving in India at the time, were disbanded on the conclusion of hostilities, but two more were raised specifically for service in India in 1787 and the renewed outbreak of war with France in 1793 saw a final wave of recruitment which brought more Highland regiments than ever before on to the Army List, some of them permanently. A few of these regiments bore entirely

new numbers, while others, confusingly, were allocated the numbers of unrelated regiments disbanded at the end of earlier conflicts.

With the exception of the two East India regiments—a new 74th and the 75th—a significant number of these regiments were raised not by career soldiers this time, but by Highland chiefs. Far from being dramatically killed off by Cumberland's guns at Culloden, the clan system survived until the end of the 18th century. While it certainly changed and gradually broke down, those changes and the ultimate breakdown, were the result of economic factors quite unconnected with Jacobitism or its violent demise. The 18th century was a period of considerable change for all of Britain, as first the agricultural and then the industrial revolutions took hold, and General Wade's roads ensured that the Highlands and its people were not insulated from these changes.

Although the roads were by no means the begetter of trade, or the most favoured routes, they facilitated the growing traffic in black cattle from the Highlands to English markets which followed the Union of 1707. This in turn had important consequences. In the first place, it transformed what was effectively a subsistence economy in which chiefs and *tacksmen* lived off the produce of their own land into a cash-based one, all the more receptive to the improving methods of agriculture being developed in the south. Secondly, in order better to effect these improvements, the landlords, whether they were Highland chiefs or the near evangelical Commissioners for Forfeited Estates, needed to alter the whole basis of landholding, replacing what were casual tenancies at will with long leases. There is no space here to examine fully either the short or long-term consequences of these changes for Highland society, but one of the more immediate effects contributed to the rise of the Highland regiments.

Whilst under the old system, a *tacksman's* tenants could be (and frequently were) shifted from

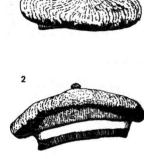

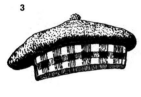

Evolution of the Highland bonnet: (1) 1740 Cloathing Book; (2) Captain John Campbell of Melfort c.1760; (3) 73rd at Gibraltar 1780; (4) Lieutenant James Stewart c.1780; (5) Dayes 1792.

farm to farm almost on an annual basis, there was always an acceptance of his obligation to provide for that tenant or follower. Not only was there a growing tendency for the superior landlord to cut out the middleman, that is, the *tacksman*, but the tenant was also being dealt with on a more business-like basis. While the long lease afforded him greater security during its term, he was at the same time rendered much more vulnerable in that there was much less of an obligation to keep him on when it expired. If he could afford the rent demanded, well and good, but if not, the landlords became increasingly willing to turn farms over to outsiders who were prepared to pay higher rents. The tenant farmer was therefore under considerable pressure to meet these spiralling rents, or to 'oblige' his landlord in other ways.

In times past, it was readily accepted that in return for the chief's protection and patronage, the clan would turn out its fighting men to march behind his banner in time of war. The Heritable

Jurisdictions Act of 1747 had removed the chief's power to demand this service, but enough of the old tradition remained for the chiefs turned landlords to expect their tenants to furnish recruits for the British Army, and for those tenants to demand concessions in return.

Captain Mackay of Bighouse may have flattered himself that his clansmen turned tenants were personally attached to him, but another of the Duke of Gordon's recruiters, Alexander Cameron of Letterfinlay, found little enthusiasm amongst his own tenants when he too tried to raise some men for the Duke's Northern Fencibles in 1778. Subsequently, he complained of one in particular, who had only enlisted under 'the utmost compulsion': '...I offered him twice in your presence to engage and I would continue him upon the same footing with the rest of the subtenants... His return always was a flat denyall upon which I have sett his lands to other people and threatened to eject him instantly; which was the only cause that induced him to serve.'

Another of the Lochaber tenants, John Cameron of Kinlochleven, was much more businesslike in his dealings with the Duke, and in May 1778, wrote to him concerning a couple of likely recruits: 'If your Grace will give me the farm of Kilmanivag and Brackletter for five years, I will furnish your Grace with two handsome men tomorrow, I would be glad to give my assistance to your Grace without those terms, but as it is not in my power to accomodate the friends of those who go, I am obliged to ask these as I have no lands of my own.'

This was plain talking indeed. Kinlochleven clearly knew of two young men who were willing to enlist if some provision was made for their dependants. If the Duke would grant him a lease of the farm, he would engage to provide for those dependants. Judging by other extant correspondence, this sort of bargaining was more common than Letterfinlay's naked threats, although it was more usually a direct contract between the

Above, recreated nine round belly-box as carried by all Highland regiments until the 1780s, and simply comprising a wooden block with a leather flap. The belt passing around the front also supported the bayonet frog.

Right, belly-box flap with stamped false gold leaf cypher of George II. Similar examples exist with George III's cypher and this may have been the single most common form of cartridge box used by the 18th century British Army.

tenant and landlord turned recruiter. A farmer named Donald McBain, for example, offered to enlist in the Fencibles in return for a new lease and the promise of being made a sergeant, while in 1794, Captain Finlason, the Duke's agent in Aberdeen (and a veteran of Morris's 89th Highlanders), reported that a former tenant named George Gordon had enlisted in the 100th (Gordon) Highlanders only on the promise of a new lease on his discharge and some provision for his wife in the meantime, as well as the usual promise of swift promotion.

Perhaps the most businesslike of all was Maclaine of Lochbuie, raising men for Allan Cameron's 79th Highlanders in February 1794: 'Major Maclaine of Lochbuy wishes to intimate to his tennants that... He will give such as enlist with him ample encouragement, such as Five Guineas Bounty or if... they hold lands on his property he will give them a deduction of thirty shillings pr. year for five years of his rent which in place of five pounds five will make his reward in money seven pounds ten shillings together with the good treatment he may expect after the Regiment is Reduced.'

In claiming that their recruits displayed a child-like devotion to them, men such as Mackay of Bighouse were inadvertently portraying them as helpless victims of an outmoded social system, a myth which is still central to John Prebble's classic study of the Highland mutinies. In reality, such residual loyalty was tempered by a hard-headed realism. While some of the loudly expressed grievances were real enough, especially when soldiers were sometimes discharged to find that promises of leases had not been kept, the vast majority of those who enlisted in the Highland regiments knew exactly what they were doing.

LAST OF THE CLAN REGIMENTS

There was another fundamental difference between the clan regiments and the regularly enlisted corps such as the Black Watch and the East Indian 74th. While the latter took recruits where they found them by the traditional method of beating up, the new regiments were raised through the exertions of men who were clan chiefs and landlords first, and military officers a long way second.

The young Marquis of Huntly was exceptional in that, unlike many of the chiefs, he actually led his 100th/92nd (Gordon) Highlanders into battle and was to be wounded doing so at Bergen in 1799. All too often, like Simon Fraser in 1775, they simply recruited their clansmen and waved them off from the quayside. In 1778, Bighouse had warned of the potential danger of appearing to abandon followers to strangers and some Highlanders did indeed complain that, having been led to believe that they would be following their own chief's banner, they were instead 'sold' to another.

While this particular grievance and other similar ones were aired in a succession of mutinies, it is highly questionable whether an imagined betrayal of old clan loyalties was entirely to blame for the subsequent disturbances. Prebble's study of the Highland mutinies is fatally flawed in taking the various incidents (most of them barely qualifying as mutinies in the first place) out of their proper context and failing to acknowledge that they were actually part of a much wider pattern of unrest, which was not confined to the Highland regiments. The sad fact of the matter is that mutiny was to some extent endemic during the British Army's periodic recruiting booms during the late 18th century. Thousands of recruits were required at short notice and could only be found by raising dozens of new battalions. It is easy to see the Highlands as being singled out for the purpose, but in the Government's eyes, there was no difference between those units proposed to be raised in the hills and more urban units backed by local corporations such as the 106th (Norwich Rangers) or the Royal Glasgow Regiment.

Nor were Highlanders alone in reacting violently

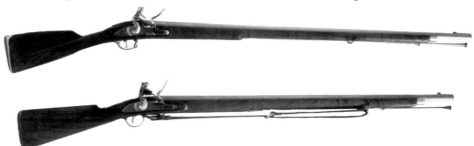

to the prospect of these mushroom regiments being disbanded and drafted into other units, as the *Morning Chronicle* noted in September 1795, when commenting on the imminent drafting of the 109th Highlanders into the 53rd Foot: 'However necessary for the public service it may be to draft men from new Regiments into old, it is much to be lamented that measures were not taken to obviate the discontents which it was easy to see it must occasion among the men who understood the terms of their enlisting to be that they should not be drafted. Nothing can be more dangerous than for the Government of a country to be suspected of breaking faith with those who are to fight in its defence. The late Mutiny of the Manchester and Birmingham Regiments in Dublin is imputable to this cause alone.'

The simple problem with the 'clan' regiments was that like all the other new corps they were levied in a hurry and in an atmosphere of cut-throat competition. The result was a severance of the last

bonds between chieftain and clansman, as potential recruits haggled over inducements. If some men extracted concessions as to rents and leases, the greater part of them simply signed up for the adventure and the biggest bounty on offer, whatever its source.

No one was in any doubt of this at the time, and where tenants were unable personally to oblige their superior in the matter of finding recruits, they could usually be relied upon to help out with some of the costs instead, as the *Aberdeen Journal* reported in April 1794: 'At a meeting of some of the Duke of Gordon's tenants in the Parish of Kirkmichael and Strathdown, it was resolved, in testimony of their gratitude and attachment to the noble family under which they and their predecessors had lived for generations, to exert themselves to assist in enlisting volunteers for the Marquis of Huntly's regiment, and for that purpose they resolved to give three guineas of additional bounty over and above every other bounty, to any

Opposite, firelocks: (top) an officer's Short Land Pattern fusil, c.1780; (bottom) a standard issue India Pattern, c.1793. Note the much heavier construction of the latter, the most widely used pattern firelock in the British Army during the Napoleonic Wars.

Above, the main gate, Fort George, Ardersier. After the fort's final completion in the 1760s, most Highland regiments were embodied here, or at Stirling, depending upon recruiting areas.

This rather crude item, excavated in America, is the earliest known pattern breast-plate belonging to the Black Watch.

J. Macalister

Passenger

Canada

good recruit from their own country, who shall voluntarily enlist with the Marquis of Huntly, or with Captain John Gordon of Coynachie, or with any of the subscribers to the present bounty for his lordship's behoof...'

Public-spirited offers of this nature were all very well, but in the end they only emphasised the degree to which even those regiments notionally associated with a clan were in the end heavily dependent upon recruiting on the open market. Worse still, by the very offering of high bounties in the first place, they were further undermining any residual ties of kinship which might remain. Where once upon a time a landless man might have followed his own clan's banner out of a sense of loyalty and duty, he was now actively encouraged to follow whichever of King George's officers had the heavier purse. What was more, an increasing number of those who took the bounty were not Highlanders at all, but Lowland Scots, Englishmen, Irishmen and even, in a few cases, foreigners.

This trend had begun much earlier with Montgomerie's cosmopolitan 77th in the old French War, and the extent of the practice varied from regiment to regiment. Sometimes, it was just a matter of picking up the odd individual, but in 1778, fully half of Campbell's 74th were raised in the Lowlands and the unprecedented demand for recruits during the long war with France between 1793 and 1815, led to a massive dilution of even the Scottish element in certain Highland regiments.

Only 390 out of the original 894 recruits who formed the 100th/92nd (Gordon) Highlanders, came from the hills and while a further 407 had the common decency to be Lowland Scots, another 51 came from Ireland and the remaining 12 were English, Welsh and German. This was by no means an isolated example and while the 78th managed to muster a very creditable 970 Highlanders out of a total of 1,103 rank and file two years later, the 79th (Cameron) Highlanders could only boast 268 Scots of any description out of 702 in 1799. It is

hardly surprising, therefore, that on 7 April 1809, the Adjutant General circulated a memorandum to the effect that: 'As the population of the Highlands of Scotland is found insufficient to supply recruits for the whole of the Highland Corps on the establishment of His Majesty's Army, and as some of these Corps, laying aside their distinguishing dress, which is objectionable to the natives of South Britain, would in a great measure tend to facilitating the completing of the establishment, as it would be an inducement to the men of the English Militia to extend their service in greater number to these regiments.'

This was the preamble to depriving six regiments of their kilts, although they would still retain the Highland designation, and while it is hard to argue with the logic of the measure, it underlines a strange paradox. By the end of the 18th century, none of the Highland battalions could truly be considered as clan regiments and, with the exception of the 78th and 93rd, they generally mustered an astonishingly high proportion of men in the ranks who were not even Highlanders, yet their character and the tactical doctrines which they were expected to espouse were widely regarded as being very different from those of the ordinary line regiments.

Opposite, although roofless cottages can be seen in this Mclan print, the Clearances did not really get underway until the 1820s and the real problem facing Highland recruiters was widespread emigration for purely economic reasons.

Right, typical militia knapsack of the Napoleonic period. The knapsack was the private property of the individual soldier and stayed with him if he volunteered into another unit. A very similar one would have been carried by Sergeant Anton, who joined the 42nd from the Aberdeenshire Militia.

HIGHLANDERS AT WAR

Opposite, Highland officer
and sergeant, early 1750s,
after Van Gucht for Grose's
Military Antiquities.
A particularly good print
with some interesting detail.
The distinctive 'serpent'
cock on the officer's fusil
is characteristic of Dublin
Castle-made weapons.

In the 76 years from the embodiment of the Black Watch as a regiment of the line in 1739, to the terrible glory of Waterloo in 1815, no fewer than 78 tartan-clad battalions of regulars or Fencibles were raised in the Highlands to justify wearing the kilt, and in that period those regiments firmly established a reputation as dashing stormers. In time, that fearsome reputation would be enhanced, sustained and eventually overwhelmed by a remarkable wave of romanticism, but initially, it was a product of official suspicions as to their reliability and the evolution of infantry fighting doctrines in the British Army.

FIREPOWER

Despite the rather casual attitude to training recounted by Stewart of Garth, it would be reasonable to suppose that the soldiers of the original Highland Independent Companies were proficient in what was termed the manual exercise—that is, their basic weapon handling—when they became the Earl of Crawford's 43rd Regiment of Foot. However, once they were embodied as a marching regiment of foot, they needed to learn the various 'evolutions', or manoeuvres, which would bring that regiment into advantageous contact with the enemy, and then they still had to master the arcane art of 'Platooning', which would enable them to destroy the enemy.

Platooning was originally devised at the beginning of the 18th century as a means of covering that vulnerable 30 seconds or so, which it took for the average soldier to reload his firelock. The earliest and simplest drills which preceded it involved deep bodies of musketeers firing by one rank at a time in the hope that, by the time all had fired in sequence, the first rank would be reloaded and ready to begin the cycle afresh. The French were still employing a variant of this technique in 1745, but the British Army was by then wedded to Platoon Firing.

Although it allowed a much shallower deployment in three and, later, in just two ranks rather than the four then being favoured by the French, the basic principle of Platooning was still broadly similar in that only a certain proportion of the men standing in the firing line were expected to be shooting at any one time. Just before the commencement of the action, the regiment's Major and his faithful assistant the Adjutant, rode down the line telling the men off into *ad hoc* Platoons, each of the same size (around 20-30 was reckoned to be the optimum), and at the same time designating which 'Firing' each Platoon was to belong to. There were a number of minor variations on the system, but when the word was given to open fire, only those Platoons assigned to the First Firing would do so, before being followed by the Platoons of the Second Firing and so on. Once again, it was assumed that if the firefight was carefully controlled, the soldiers making up the Platoons in the First Firing would have been able to reload in time to pick up the sequence after the Third or Fourth Firing. Practical experiment by re-enactors has confirmed this to be entirely feasible and, in theory, once the commanding officer had given the order to commence firing, a series of small volleys would ripple up and down the line until either a specified number of rounds had been expended, or until one side or the other gave way.

The technique looked very impressive at a formal review and perhaps even looked good on a few battlefields as well, but it was never regarded as being entirely satisfactory, particularly under the stresses of actual combat. British military thinking throughout the 18th century was largely taken up with devising a better form of Platooning. Indeed, it could be argued that since a lack of proper training facilities discouraged experimentation in grander manoeuvres, far too much attention was paid to the minutiae of Platooning. The basic arithmetic of the problem could not be altered. The common firelock could be loaded and fired twice in one minute and

the normal infantry movement rate over level ground was around 70 paces per minute. For all practical purposes, this distance was also reckoned to be the optimum effective range of the firelock. Henry Hawley referred in 1746 to 'a large Musket shot, or three score yards'—about 50 metres. Firing did frequently take place at longer distances, but beyond this comparatively short range it had little effect, except to bolster the morale of the troops who were doing the shooting. At 70 paces range, casualties could expect to be inflicted, but if the attackers could absorb those casualties and continue moving forward, there would be only time to fire into them once more before both sides came to close quarters.

It was, above all, vitally important to bring any attacking force to a halt at some point within effective killing range, but which still lay outside the distance at which one side or the other would recoil and perhaps even break and run. Once both parties were halted and blazing away at each other, the firefight would then go on until one side decided to call it a day and pulled back out of effective range. Depending upon how badly they had been hit, this could well be the moment for a vigorous advance by the victorious party, but it did not always work out that way.

Given that winning the firefight, like most other aspects of warfare, was very largely a matter of psychology, it was important to achieve three successive goals. In the first place, the initial volley or ripple of volleys needed to be heavy enough to induce the attacking force to halt and begin firing back rather than press forward into the critical zone. Secondly, tight control had to be maintained over the subsequent volleys, since any diminution in the rate of fire could encourage the enemy to come forward again and move into the critical zone. Thirdly, sufficient casualties had to be inflicted on the enemy so as to weaken his will to carry on fighting and ultimately to withdraw or even break.

That was the theory, but in practice the system suffered from two major defects. It was complicated and very easy for the various Platoons to end up firing in their own time without regard to the pre-designated sequence. If the firefight went on long enough, each soldier simply ended up loading and firing as fast as possible, without any regard for what the other members of his Platoon were doing, or for that matter where his rounds were actually going, which was usually in the air. Once this started happening, they were in trouble, especially if the other side were keeping their heads. Successive drill books, both officially sanctioned and privately published, sought to introduce improvements in the system, usually by reducing the number of Platoons and Firings. At the same time in fighting the Jacobites, another drawback became apparent.

As we have already seen, the classic Highland Charge worked by advancing straight into the critical zone as quickly as possible. Initially, Jacobite clansmen were successful in that not only was the speed of their advance deliberately pitched to be as

Charge Bayonets! This much more natural and versatile posture first appears in the 1759 *Plan of Discipline for the use of the Militia for the County of Norfolk*, although it seems to have been based on existing practice picked up from the Prussian service.

Opposite, charge your Bayonets breast High! This seemingly awkward posture is clearly based on 17th century pike drill. On the further command, Push your Bayonets!, it will be thrust forward by the right hand, which can be seen grasping the butt.

intimidating as possible, but it also minimised their own casualties and so reduced the chances of their being brought to a halt before the critical zone was breached. This in turn came about not because they were able to duck the first volley and then set about the unfortunate defenders before they had finished reloading, but because a number of small Platoons firing in sequence could not inflict enough casualties quickly enough to stop them or even to slow them down appreciably.

It also seems clear from close study of the surprising number of eyewitness accounts of Culloden, written by British soldiers, that Platooning was not employed there. Instead, the infantry reverted to the supposedly risky practice of firing by complete ranks. Hawley had in fact recommended this to his troops before Falkirk three months before: 'The sure way to demolish them is at 3 deep to fire by ranks diagonally to the Centre where they come, the rear rank first, and even that rank not to fire till they are with 10 or 12 paces.' Waiting too long also had its dangers and this instruction was subsequently modified at Culloden with the cunning refinement that the front rank immediately charged bayonets in order to protect the other two as they reloaded. This allowed them to risk opening fire earlier and thus get two full volleys in before the clansmen breached the critical zone. It is not entirely clear whether the front rank actually fired a volley of their own, or reserved their fire as was certainly the later practice when forming square against cavalry, but, either way, the result was a famous victory.

It is remarkable just how many of the British Army's more influential figures in the later 18th century fought at Culloden, as relatively junior officers, and they all of them appear to have learned two important lessons there. Firstly, there was the surprisingly obvious point that firepower was much more effective when delivered in massed volleys rather than by small Platoons, and secondly, the bayonet might have considerable potential.

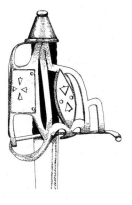

Government contract broadsword with iron hilt of Glasgow style, as issued to the rank and file of Highland regiments throughout the 18th century. In practice, it was only seen on formal parades after the 1760s.

FORWARD AT BAYONET-POINT

That potential was at first unrealised because the current bayonet drill was essentially a defensive one. Despite popular legend, it was surprisingly effective against those clansmen obliging enough to fling themselves against it, for providing the line held firm, it created a very intimidating hedge of sharp points. Even if the first bayonet was knocked aside by a targe, the very act of doing so exposed the clansman to a shrewd thrust from the second rank and the author has vivid memories of the shocked horror on the faces of some hitherto very cocky Highland re-enactors when they saw the drill demonstrated properly for the first time. On the other hand, any advance with charged bayonets necessarily involved a very slow and awkward side-step towards the enemy which was hardly calculated to put the fear of God into them. Worse still, the very slowness of the advance exposed the attackers to the prospect of taking unacceptably high casualties before breaching the critical zone. Consequently, it was reckoned much better either to press briskly forward with firelocks shouldered in a calculated display of determination, or else to simply play safe and rely on Platooning. Neither course of action was entirely satisfactory. The first could be expensive in terms of casualties, but might at least produce a quick result, while the latter could be both equally bloody and might in the long run be indecisive.

This interesting tactical problem was eventually solved, to the British Army's satisfaction at least, by two quite unrelated developments. One, which surfaced semi-officially by 1759, was the adoption of the Prussian practice of levelling the bayonet at the waist rather than breast high as before. Although it first appeared in a privately published drill-book for the Norfolk Militia, the author, William Windham, readily acknowledged the assistance and advice given by officers of the 67th and 72nd Foot, so it is likely that at least some regulars were practising it at an earlier date.

At any rate, the new style allowed the soldier to stand squarely facing the enemy and use his bayonet in a much more natural fashion—and also to move forward very briskly indeed. Levelling the bayonet at the waist permitted and encouraged a much more aggressive attitude on the battlefield. The other development was the advent of the new Highland regiments who dramatically demonstrated just what that aggressive attitude could achieve.

Despite the mutiny which followed their orders for the Continent in 1743, the Black Watch proceeded to make a notable impression on friend and foe alike in their first major action at Fontenoy on 11 May 1745, as this contemporary account relates: 'He [Sir Robert Munro] had obtained leave of the Duke of Cumberland to allow them to fight in their own way. Sir Robert, according to the usage of his countrymen, ordered the whole regiment to clap to the ground on receiving the French fire, and instantly after its discharge, they sprang up, and coming close to the enemy, poured in their shot upon them to the certain destruction of multitudes, and drove them precipitately through their own lines; then retreating drew up again, and attacked them a second time after the same manner. These attacks they repeated several times the same day, to the surprise of the whole army.'

Many secondary sources hold that the Watch executed a classic Highland Charge at Fontenoy, but it seems clear from this particular account, the most detailed available, that something more subtle was being executed. They were certainly rushing forward in the good old style, but rather than following through the one heavy volley with their broadswords, they were kept firmly in hand and pulled back to reload at a safe distance before frightening the life out of somebody else. This performance raised a few eyebrows, although Munro himself attracted just as much admiration. He appears to have been an extremely corpulent individual, and: '...it is observed, that when he commanded the whole

Print after figure in Major George Grant's *New Highland Military Discipline* (1757). Grant, a sometime officer in the Black Watch, was cashiered after a rather hasty surrender of Inverness Castle during the '45, though his fellow officers seem to have felt that he was set up.

regiment to clap to the ground, he himself alone, with the colours behind him, stood upright receiving the whole fire of the enemy; and this, because (as he said) though he could easily lie down, his great bulk would not suffer him to rise so quickly. His preservation that day was the surprise and astonishment... of the whole army.'

The novelty of the Highlanders' performance at Fontenoy was overshadowed by the outbreak of the '45 and, unfortunately, Monro, promoted to the command of the 37th Foot, was murdered by rebels at Falkirk. In 1758, the 'Old Highland Regiment', as they were then calling themselves, formed part of General Abercrombie's army,

tasked with the capture of Fort Ticonderoga as a prelude to an advance on the French colony in Upper Canada. In preparing for service in the woods, Abercrombie's infantry were ordered to strip their kit to the minimum, but the 42nd were permitted to keep their broadswords if they wished.

On 7 July, rather panicked by an unsubstantiated report that thousands of French reinforcements were approaching, Abercrombie rushed into a hasty and ill-prepared assault on the long line of field works covering the fort itself, manned by a substantial part of the French field army under the Marquis de Montcalm. His plan was less than imaginative. First to go in were the Picquets of the Day and the combined Grenadier companies, then four of his six regular battalions. The Highlanders and the 55th Foot were to form the reserve. In the hurry, the artillery was left behind and the discovery that the works were covered by a thick abattis or entanglement formed of felled oak trees, brought the whole operation to a temporary halt.

'Unexpected and disheartening as these obstructions were, the troops displayed the greatest resolution, though exposed to a most destructive fire, from an enemy well covered, and enabled to take deliberate aim, with little danger to themselves. The Highlanders, impatient at being left in the rear, could not be restrained, and rushing forward from the reserve, were soon in the front, endeavouring to cut their way through the trees with their broadswords. These weapons were here particularly useful; indeed without them, no man could have pierced through this species of defence. Much time was lost in this preliminary operation, and many men had fallen from the fire of the strong body who manned the trenches in the rear of the trees, and who retreated within the fort when the assailants penetrated the exterior defences. This destructive fire from the fort was continued with great effect. No ladders had been provided for scaling the breastwork. The soldiers were obliged to climb up on each other's shoulders, and, by

Left, two Privates of the 73rd Highlanders, as depicted by Atkinson. The 73rd was originally raised in 1780 as 2/42nd and, although the facings were changed from blue to green in 1786, they retained the red overstripe and bastion lace of the 42nd. **Private Collection**

Opposite, Recreated rear view of 42nd Royal Highland Regiment c.1790. While very attractive looking when new, the goatskin knapsack stank in wet weather and attracted flies in hot weather.

fixing their feet in the holes they had made with their swords and bayonets in the face of the work, while the defenders were so well prepared that the instant a man reached the top, he was thrown down. At length, after great exertions, Captain John Campbell with a few men, forced their way over the breastworks, but were instantly dispatched with the bayonet.'

It took three direct orders before the Highlanders would break off the assault and by the time they did retreat they had lost two-thirds of their officers and half the rank and file killed or wounded, amounting in all to no fewer than eight officers, nine sergeants and 299 killed and 17 officers, 10 sergeants and 306 men wounded. These losses temporarily crippled the regiment until it could be joined by its newly raised second battalion, but the other new Highland units proved just as impetuous. There is no doubt that, having cautiously sanctioned the recruitment of Montgomerie's 77th and Fraser's 78th in 1757, the government wanted them safely shipped out of Scotland as quickly as possible. Both regiments were posted abroad so quickly that there was no time for proper training, and, although they received some fairly elementary instruction in the manual exercise both before embarkation and while on board the transports, they landed in North America to all intents and purposes completely untrained. Ordinarily this might have had dire results and could well have led to a repeat of General Braddock's disaster on the Monongahela two years before. That particular debacle had followed the over-hasty expansion of the already inefficient 44th and 48th Foot to their wartime establishment by filling up the ranks with raw American recruits and so the equally hurried deployment of the two Highland battalions displays an alarming insouciance.

Obviously there was no question of either regiment being able to master, let alone achieve any real proficiency in Platooning under these circumstances, although by 1758 it may well have

been recognised that this was of no real consequence in the woods. More individual skills were required there and, despite an early bloody nose at Fort Duquesne (now Pittsburgh), the 77th Highlanders soon established a formidable reputation for themselves as Indian fighters. Fraser's 78th, however, were destined to face Montcalm's regulars at Quebec.

THE LAST CHARGE

In the early hours of the morning of 13 September 1759, General Wolfe's little army made its way up from the St. Lawrence River on to some open ground known as the Plains of Abraham, a little to the west of the outer defences of Quebec. Taken completely by surprise, the French reacted by mounting a hasty counter-attack without waiting for reinforcements to arrive, or even to reconnoitre properly the British position. Lieutenant Colonel Simon Fraser and his men were on the left wing of Wolfe's front line as the French commenced a vigorous but disorderly advance. Famously, the six battalions making up that line held their fire until the enemy were only 40 yards away and then they shot them to pieces in short order. There is some continuing dispute as to whether their musketry took the form of just one 'perfect volley', as described in Sir John Fortescue's magisterial history, or the 'regular Platooning' mentioned by some more contemporary sources. The former would obviously explain the way in which the French were brought to an abrupt halt, but it is equally possible that each individual regiment regulated its fire according to its own proficiency and there is no evidence that Fraser's 78th attempted Platooning. On the contrary, after a heavy volley brought the regiments of *La Sarre* and *Languedoc* lurching to a confused halt, 'the Highlanders taking to their broadswords fell in among them with irresistible impetuosity, and drove them back with great slaughter.'

It is often claimed that some recruits for the 84th

Left, the 1828 pattern Highland officer's broadsword. The basket hilt has been reversed in this photograph in order to illustrate better the ring linking the bars at the top.

Right, the broadsword's nemesis–the Land Pattern bayonet–17" of fluted steel.

(Royal Highland Emigrants) attempted to launch a similar charge at Moore's Creek Bridge, North Carolina in 1776, vainly crying 'King George and Broadswords!'. Although the men who led that particular assault were indeed armed with broadswords, the attack very quickly came to grief in attempting to scramble over the half-demolished bridge. There never was a Highland Charge as such at the Widow Moore's creek and the credit for launching the last charge in the old style with broadswords rather than bayonets must still rest with Fraser and his renegade Jacobites at Quebec in 1759.

This was undoubtedly a reflection on the rapidly changing character of the Highland regiments themselves. In 1768, an annual inspection report on the 42nd noted that with the exception of the Grenadier company, all their broadswords had been left in store. At a subsequent inspection in 1775, the commanding officer, Lieutenant Colonel Thomas Stirling, explained the omission by stating that 'the Highlanders on several occasions declined using broadswords in America, that they all prefer bayonets, and that swords for the Battalion men, though part of their dress and establishment are incumbrances.'

Similarly the equally distinctive Highland pistols began to disappear at about the same period. For a long time it seems that they were treated as no more than a perquisite for the regimental colonels, who purchased them at a lower rate than the government allowed and pocketed the difference. In 1761, suspicious officials were even moved to demand proof that Colonel Campbell of the 88th had actually bought any at all, and the weapon was officially withdrawn from the rank and file of

Sir James Grant of Grant, Highland Chieftain and successively Colonel of the 1st or Strathspey Fencibles and the 97th (Inverness-shire) Regiment. He is depicted here by John Kay in the uniform of the former.

Captain John Rose of Holm, a rather portly officer serving in the 1st or Strathspey Fencibles. Although it was a Highland regiment, there is nothing at all in Rose's uniform to identify it as such. Many Highland officers wore similar uniforms in the 1790s.

Highland regiments in 1776.

Both weapons had been 'established' when the original Highland Watch was embodied as a marching regiment in 1739. At that time, by far the greater number of the rank and file were, for want of a better term, Highland Gentlemen who were accustomed to carrying both sword and pistols. Indeed, the privilege of carrying them openly was widely reckoned to be a major incentive to enlistment in the Watch in the first place. By the 1750s, the Highland regiments, with the possible exception of Fraser's 78th, were no longer composed of Highland Gentlemen and a significant number of soldiers in the ranks were not even Highlanders at all. Whilst the new recruits may initially have been flattered to be issued with gentlemen's weapons, they were neither by tradition nor practice accustomed to carrying or using them. Like the early volunteers who marched off to fight in the American Civil War laden down with revolvers and huge Bowie knives, they soon decided that they were 'incumbrances' and just as quickly discarded them to carry just a firelock and bayonet.

This is not to say that the 'new' Highlanders no longer followed the old tactics of firing a single volley and then rushing forward in what they fondly hoped was an intimidating manner. They could hardly do otherwise, for just as the 77th and 78th were hastily shipped overseas without adequate training, so were all too many of those which followed them. In Germany, for example, Keith's 87th Highland Volunteers did very well in their first action at Eibelshausen in 1759, which according to Stewart of Garth 'was the more remarkable as they were no other than raw recruits just arrived from their own country, and altogether unacquainted with regular discipline.'

It was also the case with Simon Fraser's other regiment, the two-battalion 71st Highlanders, which he raised in 1775: 'Could an hypothesis be grounded on a few facts, Fraser's Highlanders would prove that men without discipline, depending entirely on their native spirit and energy, are capable of performing, in the most perfect manner, every duty of a soldier. Few British regiments ever went into immediate service with less discipline than this regiment, except Keith's and Campbell's Highlanders in Germany... without any training, except what they got on board the transport from non-commission officers, nearly as ignorant as themselves, these men were brought into action at Brooklyn, and on no future occasion, even after the experience of six campaigns, did they display more spirit or soldier-like conduct... Such indeed, were the constant and active duties, and incessant marching, actions and changes of quarters of the 71st, that little time could be spared; and, therefore, little attempt was made to give them the polish of parade discipline till the third year of the war. Field discipline, and forcing their enemy to fly wherever they met him, (except on two occasions, when the fault lay not with them,) they understood perfectly...'.

The nature of that field discipline was described elsewhere by Lieutenant Colonel John Groves Simcoe, a regular officer who commanded an American Loyalist corps called the Queen's Rangers: 'A Light corps, augmented as the Queen's Rangers was, and employed in the duties of an outpost, had no opportunity of being instructed in the general discipline of the army, nor indeed was it necessary: the most important duties, those of vigilance, activity and patience of fatigue, were best learnt in the field; a few motions of the manual exercise were thought sufficient; they were carefully instructed in those of firing, but above all, attention was paid to inculcate the use of the bayonet, and a total reliance on that weapon.'

It was enough to make Humphrey Bland, whose *Treatise of Military Discipline* had for so long formed the basis of British infantry tactics, turn in his grave, but in sober truth there was little alternative. The British Army which won the battle of Culloden had nearly 30 years solid peacetime

Recreated Private 42nd with white fatigue jacket, a useful illustration showing how high the early kilt came up the body. At this period, it was box pleated and fastened by pins or small buttons, rather than modern straps and buckles.

Opposite, Recreated rear view of a Private 42nd Royal Highland Regiment c.1800. His knapsack identifies him as a volunteer from the 1st or Strathspey Fencibles.

experience behind it. Examination of the Chelsea Hospital records reveals that those men who were wounded there and at the earlier battle of Falkirk were generally old sweats in their thirties and forties who had practised Platooning for years. In fact, given the lack of proper barrack facilities and consequent dispersion of troops, it is likely that they had the opportunity to practise little else. As these veterans died or were pensioned off, they were replaced by younger men, lacking that single-minded experience, and by a succession of newly raised regiments with no experience at all. Given the remarkable expansion of the army during the Seven Years War and in the subsequent American War of Independence, it is scarcely surprising that there was a decline in the quality of the infantry and a corresponding need to devise a simpler tactical system better suited to changing conditions.

LOOSE FILES AND AMERICAN SCRAMBLE

During the American War of Independence, a distinct split emerged between those units stationed at home (including Highland ones like Gordon's 81st) and the 'Americans'. The former were still being trained and exercised according to the official 1764, and later 1779 *Regulations*, both of which stressed the primacy of Platooning. Men such as Simcoe developed what was sneeringly derided by conservative critics as 'loose files and American scramble'.

It was a fairly heretical tactical doctrine which was derived at least in part from Highland practice. Essentially, the idea was simply to march straight up to the enemy, fire one volley and then advance through the smoke with levelled bayonets. With fire discipline no longer all-important, it was possible to sacrifice solidity for mobility and with some few exceptions it was pretty successful. Traditionalists such as the immensely influential David Dundas argued that, while it might work well enough in America, Continental conditions were very different, as indeed they may have been when he committed

his *Principles of Military Movements* to paper. The long war against Revolutionary and Napoleonic France, which began in 1793, did, however, see the gradual ascendancy of the American school. The famous (and quite unjustly maligned) 'Eighteen Manoeuvres', originally set out in Dundas' *Principles*, served as an indispensable foundation, but, increasingly, the British Army's tactical doctrines saw responsibility for maintaining the sustained firefight pass from the solidly formed line of battalion companies to the ever thicker screen of skirmishers deployed in front of it. The role of the formed companies was, as in America, to deliver a heavy volley at the critical moment and then follow it up with a bayonet charge.

Consequently, even as late as the Napoleonic Wars, something of the old rough and ready spirit survived in the Highland regiments. James Anton, a weaver from Huntly who volunteered from the Aberdeenshire Militia into the 42nd, recalled that the Black Watch held to it in the Pyrenees and afterwards at Waterloo: 'First the ruggedness of the mountains prevented precision of movements; secondly the weather had become so unfavourable that every fair day was dedicated to some necessary purpose about the camp, and instead of acquiring practical knowledge himself [the CO, Lieutenant Colonel Macara], even his regiment was losing part of that which it had perhaps previously possessed; thirdly, drafts of undisciplined recruits were occasionally joining and mixing in the ranks, and being unaccustomed to field movements, occasioned a sort of awkwardness in the performance of them. Even after our return from the Continent, when the regiment was quartered in Ireland, many obstacles started up unfavourable to field practice, namely old soldiers and limited service men being discharged, the second battalion joining, the principal part of which were recruits, and men who had been years in French prisons; the detached state of the regiment, after all these had been squad drilled, left but few soldiers at headquarters to enable the commanding officer to practise with. In this manner we continued until the battle of Waterloo... We had the name of a crack corps, but certainly it was not then in the state of discipline which it could justly boast of a few years afterwards.'

It sounds reminiscent of descriptions of the old 71st in the American War of Independence, or Colonel Simcoe's Rangers, and although many other British units in the Peninsula must have been in the same condition, it is unlikely that they viewed the situation with the same equanimity as the Highland ones. On the other hand, whilst their proficiency in drill (or at least manoeuvring, for there is no suggestion that their weapon handling was deficient) may not have been all that could be

asked for, Highland regiments could still be as steady as any other when required to stand on the defensive and the now forgotten fight by the 92nd (Gordon) Highlanders on the heather-covered ridge at Maya in 1813 provides a good example of this.

By midsummer 1813, after Wellington's great triumph at Vittoria, the French armies had been substantially driven out of Spain. Only a few beleaguered garrisons remained and the British Army was firmly established in the Pyrenean passes. Then, at the end of July, a new Imperial commander, Marshal Soult, launched a sudden counter-attack across the mountains, aimed at relieving the French garrison in Pamplona. Early on the morning of 25 July, one of his corps led by General D'Erlon began pushing through the

Death of Colonel Macara of the 42nd at Quatre Bras, after Captain Jones. Already wounded, the Colonel was being taken to the rear when he and his carrying party were murdered by some Polish lancers.

Col de Maya. At 10.30, the light companies of Darmagnac's Division surprised the British outposts. The British commander, Major General William Stewart, known to his men as 'Auld Grog Wullie', was absent, but the senior brigadier, Pringle, brought up his own brigade and began calling up elements of a second under Lieutenant Colonel John Cameron of Fassifern. As the French piled on the pressure, Pringle's men were pushed southwards, away from the all-important road known as the *Chemin des Anglais*, which ran along the ridge-top.

At this juncture, just as Pringle's counter-attack was failing, the right wing of Cameron's own regiment, the 92nd (Gordon) Highlanders came up and with the 28th Foot on their flank formed across the *Chemin* and advanced towards the French. The ridge was barely 50 metres wide at this point and there was no attempt at a wild charge with bayonets. Instead, less than 400 Highlanders drew up in two ranks and for an incredible 20 minutes

fought a whole French division to a bloody standstill. The most moving description of the fight came from Sir George Bell's *Rough Notes*: 'The 92nd were in line pitching into the French like blazes, and tossing them over. They stood there like a stone wall overmatched by twenty to one, until half their blue bonnets lay beside those brave northern warriors. When they retired their dead bodies lay as a barrier to the advancing foe. Oh but they did fight well that day; I can still see now the line of killed and wounded stretched upon the heather, as the living retired, closing to the centre.'

The casualties were horrific; two sergeants and 32 men were killed and no fewer than 19 officers, 10 sergeants and 258 men wounded. Some of them belonged to the largely unengaged left wing and others may have fallen during the final counter-attack, but the greater part of them were killed or wounded during the stand on the ridge. At length, the senior of the two surviving officers ordered them to retire, and at 2pm Stewart finally turned up and pulled everyone back to a final stop position south of the *Chemin des Anglais*. Once that position was forced, the French would win clear of the pass, but they too were exhausted by now and before they could organise a proper attack, elements of the British 7th Division came barrelling westwards along the *Chemin* and piled into the French flank. Recognising his opportunity, Stewart counter-attacked again and, according to the Gordons' historian, they too went forward: 'General Stewart, having regard to the extraordinary loss and fatigue sustained by them, desired that the 92nd should not join in the charge of Barnes' troops, but this time the pipe-major was not to be denied. He struck up the charging tune of *The Haughs of Cromdale*, his comrades, seized with what in the Highlands is called "Mire chath"—the Frenzy of Battle—without either asking or obtaining permission, not only charged, but led the charge, and rushed down on the enemy with irresistible force, driving back their opponents in the most splendid style.'

Left, recreated Private 42nd Royal Highland Regiment in full marching order c1810. The earlier folding knapsack has now been replaced by the black-painted envelope or 'Trotter' style.

Opposite, recreated Private 42nd Royal Highland Regiment c.1810.

By any standards, it was a notable fight, but that last 'splendid' flourish aside, it did not accord with what were already preconceived notions of how Highland soldiers behaved, and it was soon forgotten. The rather better publicised defensive action by the 93rd at Balaklava in 1854 may not have fitted in with public preconceptions either, but it was recorded for posterity in a famous newspaper report and later in a still more famous painting. When artists turned to the Gordons for inspiration they found it not on the *Chemin des Anglais*, but in the so-called stirrup charge at Waterloo.

WATERLOO

Captain William Siborne related what has come to be the accepted version of the Highland Charge at Waterloo in his 1844 *History of the Waterloo Campaign*, which was itself based on a mass of correspondence gathered from veterans. Sir Denis Pack's brigade was coming under severe pressure from D'Erlon's French division and, according to a number of accounts, was on the point of breaking, when Ponsonby's heavy cavalry brigade came up to their support and charged through intervals opened up in the ranks of the 42nd and 92nd Highlanders: 'As the Scots Greys passed through, and mingled with the Highlanders, the enthusiasm of both corps was extraordinary. They mutually cheered. "Scotland for ever!" was their war-shout. The smoke in which the head of the French column was enshrouded had not cleared away, when the Greys dashed into the mass. So eager was the desire, so strong the determination, of the Highlanders to aid their compatriots in completing the work so

71st Highland Light Infantry in action at Waterloo, after Captain Jones. Note that the piper is wearing an ordinary soldier's uniform rather than Highland dress, although he does have a short musician's sword.

gloriously begun, that many were seen holding on by the stirrups of the horsemen, while all rushed forward, leaving none but the disabled in their rear.'

Stirring stuff, but while eyewitness accounts describe how only a comparatively small number of Highlanders went forward, there was no doubt that at least some of them did and the traditional story is confirmed in the narrative written by one of the troopers of the Greys: 'Our Colonel shouted out: "Now then, Scots Greys, Charge!" and waving his sword in the air he rode straight at the hedges in front which he took in grand style. At once a great cheer rose from our ranks and we waved our swords and followed him. I drove my spurs into my brave old Rattler and we were off like the wind. It was a grand sight to see the long line of grey horses dashing along with manes flowing and heads down, tearing the turf about them as they went. The men in their red coats and tall bearskins were cheering wildly and the trumpets were sounding the charge. We heard the pipes of the Ninety-Second playing in the smoke, and I plainly saw my old friend Pipe Major Cameron standing apart on a hillock coolly playing "Hey Johnnie Cope, are ye waking yet?" in all the din. All of us were greatly excited and began crying out, "Hurrah, Ninety-Second! Scotland for ever!" Many of the Highlanders grasped our stirrups, and in the fiercest excitement dashed with us into the fight.'

No doubt there about the two regiments charging together, but, although it sounds a touch romanticised, a sergeant of the Gordons, who was evidently in the fight afterwards, wrote that 'it was fearful to see the carnage that took place. The dragoons were lopping off heads at every stroke, while the French were calling for quarter. We were also among them busy with the bayonet and what the cavalry did not execute we completed.' On the other hand, Stewart of Garth, ever ready to garner laurels for the Highland regiments, merely alludes to the charge, without mentioning anything of stirrups, and while Lieutenant Robert Winchester's

account states that at least some of the 92nd went forward with the Greys, he makes no mention of men actually hanging on to the cavalrymen's stirrups either.

When all is said and done, it is unlikely that we will ever know the whole truth about that charge. Critical modern historians have been quick to pour scorn on the story and cast doubt on the very practicality of their doing so in the first place, but they all of them belong to a generation which is fundamentally unfamiliar with horses. The story emerged at or very shortly after Waterloo and for a century and more it was firmly believed by men who grew up with horses and spent their working lives with horses. Yet none of them claimed that the feat was physically impossible or even unlikely, and there was even a doubtful claim in some newspapers that the Black Watch and the Greys had emulated it in an incident during the retreat from Mons in 1914. The point by then was not a question of whether a 'stirrup charge' actually happened, for whether the Gordons actually held on to the troopers stirrups as they went forward is immaterial, but that it was the sort of action expected of Highlanders and that people wanted to believe that it had happened.

BRAVE HIGHLAND MEN

The Highland regiments were set apart in the popular mind from the more stolid regiments of the line and in 1828 Thomas Creevey happily noted in his diary: 'We have an event in our family. Fergy [Lieutenant General Sir Ronald Craufurd Ferguson] has got a regiment—a tip top crack one—one of those beautiful Highland Regiments that were at Brussels, Quatre Bras and Waterloo.'

Why Ferguson's command of the 79th (Cameron) Highlanders should have been regarded as quite such a plum is an interesting question. Other regiments, such as the Connaught Rangers, were certainly their equal in dash and daring on the battlefield, but a combination of factors ensured the

Highlanders would stand out as something different.

In the first place, they personified a quite remarkable wave of romanticism which followed the destruction of the last Jacobite army at Culloden. For generations, clansmen had been demonised and despised by their southern neighbours, but once they no longer posed a threat to the stability of the Kingdom or to the maintenance of law and order, attitudes changed. The 'invention' of Highland romanticism is generally laid at the door of Sir Walter Scott, and to Colonel David Stewart of Garth, whose *Sketches of the Highlanders of Scotland* was published in 1822. But, while both men more than played their part, it really began much earlier with James MacPherson's *Ossian*. Purportedly a rendering of ancient oral traditions, *Ossian* was an epic tale of Celtic heroes and if it was indeed a forgery, as is generally supposed, it still faithfully reflected a semi-mythical world which both Highlanders and their new-found admirers wanted to believe in.

MacPherson's heroes could just as easily been Irish, but the nationalist revival in that country was still some way in the future and would come in time to be tainted with Fenianism. The Scottish Highlanders, on the other hand, had a clear pedigree. Even if the Ossianic tales were a fabrication, or at best an embroidering of half forgotten legends, they related to a people and a way of life which had still been extant within living memory. Moreover, whilst there was apparently nothing but his brogue to mark the Irishman, MacPherson's Ossianic heroes still visibly walked on the earth in the shape of the kilted regiments raised in the hills and, more particularly, in the swaggeringly extravagant behaviour of men such as the young Glengarry, who consciously acted out these Celtic fantasies and served as a living model for Sir Walter Scott's own generation of Highland paladins.

While the growth of romanticism in the latter half of the 18th century and its yet more exuberant

Opposite, Waterloo, 2.30pm, 18 June, 1815. **This reconstruction, based on Captain Jones' near contemporary sketch, depicts the celebrated charge by the 92nd (Gordon) Highlanders and the 2nd (Royal North British) Dragoons, the Scots Greys, at Waterloo. Both regiments are wearing service dress; the Greys with oilskin covers on their bearskins and folded saddle blankets rather than elaborate shabraques.**

The grenadiers of the 92nd provide an excellent illustration of the way in which Highland dress was adapted to the needs of the British Army. The bulky belted plaid has given way to the kilt, which at this period is still a relatively simple box-pleated garment. The tartan is the old Government or Black Watch sett with the addition of a single yellow overstripe by way of distinction. A lighter-toned version of this military sett, originally devised for the 6th (Northern) Fencibles in 1793, will eventually become recognised as the Gordon clan tartan. The old flat blue bonnet is now only worn in undress and has instead been replaced by the relatively tall drum-shaped Kilmarnock bonnet, with a decorative diced band mirroring the red and white checked hose. The Jacket is slightly shorter than those worn by ordinary regiments of the line, with only eight buttons on the front rather than the usual 10, but is otherwise no different.

The same is true of the officer's uniform. The double-breasted jacket is of conventional cut and, as usual in this period, is fully fastened over, rather than leaving the top three buttons undone in order to reveal the facing coloured lining. This practice only appears to have become common throughout the Army after the general adoption of jackets instead of long-tailed coats by line infantry in 1812, but a number of portraits suggest that Highland officers had been fastening their jackets much earlier. Also typical is the wearing of grey trousers rather than the kilt on active service. Even from the very earliest times, Highland officers displayed an interesting reluctance to wear the kilt. In part, this might well be a hangover from the days when gentlemen made a point of wearing trews and riding rather than walking--and officers of all ranks normally rode on the march during the Peninsular War--but the kilt does genuinely seem to have been unpopular. When the officers of the Reay Fencibles were instructed to parade in Highland dress, instead of their customary breeches and round hats, they reacted with some consternation as none of them possessed it.

The colour which appears in the background is that of the regiment's 2nd Battalion, distinguished as such by the broad red band running horizontally across it. The 2nd Battalion was disbanded in 1814 without having seen service, other than garrison duty in Ireland, but there is reason to believe that this colour was actually carried by the 1st Battalion at Waterloo since its own was in an extremely tattered condition after hard service in the Peninsula. *Painting by Graham Turner.*

flowering in the Victorian era very largely conditioned how Highland regiments were seen by an admiring public, it would be a mistake to dismiss their formidable reputation as being no more than an artificially created and cynically sustained myth. Highland regiments were, and still are, different for reasons which are much more fundamental than that.

Soldiering was always regarded in a much more respectable light in the north of Scotland then elsewhere in Britain. There was no stigma attached to going for a soldier and the quality of the recruits was consequently higher than average, with a fair leavening of respectable tenant farmers' sons amongst the usual collection of unemployed and unemployable tradesmen, weavers and landless labourers. The composition of the Highland regiments tended to be much more homogenous, since both the initial and subsequent quotas of recruits came from broadly the same areas and often from the same families as well. To a rather greater extent than in the line, the commissioned officers also came from those same areas and just as frequently brought with them recruits from their own or their fathers' farms and estates. While they certainly were not 'clan' regiments, both officers and men often strove to behave as if they were, and this despite the often strong presence of Lowland Scots, Irishmen and even a few Englishmen in the ranks. There was a much closer, happier and more efficient bond between officers and men in the Highland regiments, which in turn meant fewer disciplinary problems and higher morale. According to Stewart of Garth, the Light Company of the 1/93rd (Sutherland) Highlanders had not a single man punished in the 20 years since it was embodied in 1800. Whilst this was obviously an exceptional case, there is no doubting that it reflected an accepted standard of behaviour unknown in non-Highland units.

The regiments' very distinctive Highland dress and the kilt, expensive as it was, also helped to foster and sustain the ordinary soldier's belief that he was part of something special, and in the eyes of outsiders, the kilt instantly distinguished Highland corps from the rest of the army. By the time of the Napoleonic Wars, most British regiments were dressed alike and generally identified one from another only by the contrasting 'facing colours' on the collar and cuffs of their red jackets. As the 19th century wore on, even these small distinctions disappeared, to be replaced by the universal drabness of khaki, but throughout the years of empire and the bloodbath of the First World War which followed, the Highland regiments remained instantly recognisable through their kilts, bonnets and bagpipes.

Not surprisingly, non-kilted regiments were apt to complain, as they did after the fight at Dargai on India's North-West Frontier, that if a kilted regiment was present it would automatically attract all the glory, no matter what other, more anonymous units did to earn it the hard way. While this was undoubtedly true, there was another side to the coin in that bearing a proud reputation as stormers, regiments such as the Gordons considered themselves obliged to maintain that reputation at whatever the cost in blood and lives. Notwithstanding the grim resistance on the ridge at Maya, or the rather briefer glory of the 'thin red streak' above Balaklava, the bayonet charge was the way in which Highland regiment were expected to fight. This tradition undoubtedly had its destructive side in sometimes leading to unnecessarily high casualties, but in the end it was also that proud reputation which sustained the regulars, territorials, Kitchener volunteers and conscripts of the Highland battalions through the long-drawn out horror of the Western Front.

Stewart of Garth closed his own history of the Highlanders by recalling how he had often heard the mothers and sisters of recruits consoling themselves with the words: 'Well, if I should never see his face again, he is a companion to brave soldiers and honourable men: he belongs to the Black Watch.'

Opposite, this magnificent but ultimately unconvincing print by Mclan is the very embodiment of the romantic ideal of the Highland warrior, which served as an inspiration for men such as Private William Grant of the Gordon Highlanders.

A country postman from the Lowlands of Aberdeenshire, Wullie Grant was typical of the men who served in the Highland regiments in the muddy horror of the Western Front. Loss of an arm there did not prevent him from winning ploughing matches after the war.

![Military Illustrated masthead](MILITARY ILLUSTRATED)

Military Illustrated is the leading monthly military history magazine in the English language. Since its inception, it has built up an unrivalled reputation among military historians, enthusiasts, collectors, re-enactors, and military modellers for authoritative articles, primary research, rare photographs, and specially commissioned artwork spanning the entire history of warfare from ancient to modern – including the most popular periods such as World Wars Two and One, Napoleonic Wars, and ancient and medieval combat.

Copies of the magazine are available on newsstands and in specialist shops or can be obtained directly from the publisher on subscription from:

Military Illustrated
45 Willowhayne Avenue
East Preston
West Sussex
BN16 1PL
Great Britain
Tel: 01903 775121

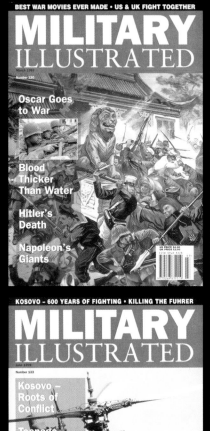

APPENDIX

HIGHLAND REGIMENTAL HISTORIES

During the 18th century, many Highland regiments were formed, disbanded and sometimes re-formed. This leads to considerable confusion which can only be eliminated by examining them in chronological fashion. Most Highland regiments raised during the 18th century had a brief existence. Generally they were hastily recruited at the outset of each successive crisis and then either just as hastily disbanded or at best renumbered when peace came.

As a result, in the period between 1745 and 1792, there were, amongst others, two 71st, two 73rd, two 74th, two 77th and two 78th Highland Regiments, and yet a third 78th raised in 1793.

In order to avoid this confusion, regiments are identified by the number or designation which they actually bore during a particular conflict. Some units survived to fight in more than one war, with or without an alteration in their designation, but the notes on their services and uniforms are confined to what is actually known to have been worn during the period in question.

By way of a general comment on clothing and equipment it should be noted that, until about 1760, Highlanders of all ranks wore short single-breasted jackets. These were collar-less in the 1740s, but thereafter acquired a small turn-down collar in the regimental facing colour. Officers wore the same jacket, sometimes with lapels, though these may have been confined to field officers. Lapels were more generally worn by officers after 1760 and perhaps by the rank and file as well, although evidence is lacking on this. In 1768 both officers and men adopted the same pattern jacket worn by the light companies of line regiments.

Bonnets were invariably knitted and flat in shape until the 1770s, when there was a very gradual introduction of the cocked 'Kilmarnock' style bonnet, with a diced band. Tartans were primarily of the government sett, more commonly known as the Black Watch sett. Some regiments raised in the 1740s and 1750s had quite distinctive tartans, but by the 1770s all units appear to have used the government sett as a base and added coloured overstripes by way of distinction.

WAR OF THE AUSTRIAN SUCCESSION 1743-1748

43rd Highland Regiment

Embodied from independent companies as the 43rd Foot in 1739/40. It served in Germany and Flanders in 1743-45, most notably at Fontenoy, before being stationed in southern England during the Jacobite crisis of 1745/6. Afterwards it took part in the L'Orient raid, before again serving in Flanders from 1747 to 1748. Three additional companies, which were recruiting in Scotland in 1745, effectively formed a 2nd Battalion serving there throughout the rebellion and after, until reduced in 1748. The original companies were sent to Ireland in 1749 and re-numbered as the 42nd.

Uniform: Short red jackets and waistcoats. Yellow buff facings. Gold braid for officers. No ORs lace shown in 1742 Clothing Book, but the Morier grenadier painting of 1748 or 1749 shows pointed-end loops with a double red line. The tartan was originally an undifferenced government sett, but a red overstripe was added in 1746 for all companies, probably in order to differentiate them from the Highland independent companies raised during the rebellion.

64th (Loudon's) Highlanders

Raised in 1745 by John Campbell, Earl of Loudon. Served in Scotland 1745/46 in detached companies, one of which, commanded by Captain Colin Campbell of Ballimore, fought at Culloden. All of the companies were at last properly embodied in 1747 and sent to Flanders. There the regiment took part in the unsuccessful defence of Bergen-op-Zoom and was disbanded in 1748.

Uniform: Short red jackets, red or tartan waistcoats, two officers' portraits show red tartan ones. White or dove grey facings. Gold braid for officers. Red tartan sett identical to modern Stuart of Bute sett, or at least something very similar indeed. The portraits (Loudon himself and Lieutenant John Reid) show that belts and equipment were buff rather than the black leather normally worn by Highland regiments throughout the 18th century.

THE SEVEN YEARS' WAR 1756-1763

42nd Highland Regiment

Originally embodied in 1739/40 as the 43rd Foot, but renumbered in 1749 and generally referred to thereafter as the 'Old Highland Regiment'. Sent to New York in 1756. Took part in unsuccessful attempt on Louisburg 1757 and on Ticonderoga 1758. Created 'Royal Highland Regiment' in 1758 and 2nd Battalion authorised at the same time which it served on Martinique and Guadaloupe in 1759 before joining 1st Battalion. Both battalions were at the taking of Martinique and the Havannah in 1762, then returned to North America where they fought at Bushy Run. The 2nd Battalion was reduced in 1763 and the 1st returned to Ireland in 1767.

Uniform: Buff facings changed to dark blue in 1758. The pointed lace loops appear to have been altered to a 'flowerpot' bastion shape circa 1760. Tartan for all companies was the government sett with a red overstripe. Kilts were apparently worn by the 2nd Battalion on Guadaloupe in 1759, but regimental orders also show *mitasses* (Indian leggings) and sometimes breeches worn in North America by the 1st Battalion.

77th (Montgomerie's) Highlanders

Raised in 1757 as 1st Highland Regiment and briefly numbered 62nd. Served in North America – in New York and the Carolinas, and at the taking of Martinique and the Havannah in 1762. The Light Company and one other (both left behind in North America) took part in the recapture of St Johns, Newfoundland, in 1762. A contingent also fought at Bushy Run. Disbanded in 1763.

Uniform: Facings may originally have been red but were certainly green by 1761 when described in a local Army List. Silver braid worn by officers, no lace pattern appears to be recorded for ORs. Tartan was also unrecorded but probably the undifferenced government sett.

78th (Fraser's) Highlanders

Raised in Inverness-shire in 1757 as '2nd Highland Regiment' and briefly numbered 63rd. Served in North America, most notably at the taking of Quebec in 1759, and two companies were also at the recapture of St Johns, Newfoundland. Disbanded in 1763.

Uniform: White or more likely very pale buff facings – not unlike those once worn by the Seaforth Highlanders. A portrait of an unknown officer of the regiment by William Delacour shows unlaced jackets. Tartan appears from this and other paintings to have been an unidentified reddish brown sett, though it is possible that initially at least each company may have had its own sett.

87th (Keith's) Highlanders

Raised partially in Lowland Aberdeenshire in 1759. Served with some distinction in Germany as part of British Grenadier Brigade, mostly notably at Warburg and Kloster Kamp. Disbanded in 1763.

Uniform: Bright green facings are shown in two portraits – Colonel Keith and Captain John Gorrie. Gold braid for officers arranged in Gorrie's case in alternate pear-shaped and bastion loops;

no lace pattern seems to be recorded for ORs. Tartan appears from both portraits to have been the undifferenced government sett, but with a quite distinct greenish tinge.

88th (Campbell's) Highlanders

Raised in 1760 from a nucleus of officers and men drawn from the 87th. Served alongside them in Germany and effectively comprised a second battalion of the 87th. Disbanded in 1763.

Uniform: No details known but facings were probably green as for the 87th and an undifferenced government sett worn.

89th (Morris's) Highlanders

Raised in Aberdeenshire in 1759 with an unusually high proportion (for the time) of Lowland Scots recruits. Served in India 1761-1764, most notably at Buxar. Disbanded in 1765.

Uniform: Light yellow facings. Silver braid for officers, no lace pattern recorded for ORs. Tartan was probably the undifferenced government sett.

100th (Campbell's) Highlanders

Embodied in 1761 from various independent companies. Initially sent to the Channel Islands but later took part in the capture of Martinique in 1762. Disbanded in 1763.

Uniform: No details are known although the facings were probably the yellow ones customarily allocated to Argyllshire units.

101st (Johnstone's) Highlanders

Embodied in 1761 from independent companies (mainly raised in Perthshire). Originally intended for service in Germany but in the end it effectively acted as a depot battalion, supplying drafts for the 87th and 88th Highlanders. Disbanded in 1763.

Uniform: Pale yellowish buff facings, otherwise no details are known.

105th (Queen's) Highlanders

Two battalions raised in 1761. Served in Ireland until disbanded in 1763.

Uniform: Sky-blue facings. Gold braid for officers, no lace pattern recorded for ORs. Tartan as shown in the striking portrait of Lieutenant-Colonel William Gordon of Fyvie, appears to have been an unidentified blue and red sett.

114th (Maclean's or Royal Highland Volunteers)

Letters of service for this unit were granted in October 1761 and it seems to have been intended for service in North America, but only six companies had been raised by the end of the war and it saw no service before being disbanded.

Uniform: Dark blue facings, silver braid for officers. Tartan was probably the undifferenced government sett.

AMERICAN WAR OF INDEPENDENCE 1775-1783

1/42nd Royal , Highland Regiment

Sent to North America in 1776; fought at Long Island (temporarily reorganised into two battalions) and in the Jerseys, at Brandywine, Paoli's Tavern, Germantown (Light Company only) Billingsport, White Marsh and Monmouth, Thereafter in New York garrison, except for taking part in the capture of Charleston in 1780. The Light Company, however, served at Yorktown in the composite Light Infantry battalion, a sergeant and five men are returned as having been killed there. Subsequently served in Canada 1783-1789.

2/42nd Royal Highland Regiment

Raised in 1780 and sent to India in the following year. Served in the south against Haider Ali and his son, Tippoo Sahib, most notably in the defence of Bangalore. Became 73rd Highlanders in 1786.

Uniform (both battalions): Dark blue facings. Gold braid for officers arranged in square-end loops. There is a reference to a Sergeant McPherson wearing silver braid. ORs had white lace, with a single red line on the outside, arranged in 'flowerpot' bastion loops; these were changed to 'Jews Harp' bastions by 1792. Stewart of Garth, who joined the regiment in 1787, states quite categorically that the plaids were at this time made from the undifferenced government sett, while the same sett with the red overstripe was used for kilts. White trousers or pantaloons were worn by both battalions on active service, officers in white breeches and stockings.

71st (Fraser's) Highlanders

Two Battalions were raised in 1775 and hastily sent to North America in the following year; fought at Long island (temporarily reorganised into three battalions), Brandywine, Billingsport, Savannah, Augusta, Savannah (again), Charieston, Camden, Cowpens, Guilford Courthouse, Green Spring and Yorktown. A detachment was still in Charleston at the end of the war. Disbanded in 1783.

Uniform: White facings. Silver braid for officers, and white lace with a red worm for ORs, arranged in paired square-end loops. Tartan was the undifferenced government sett. Plain blue bonnets were originally specified and supplied, but a portrait of Major Duncan McPherson of Cluny (Ist Battalion) shows a Kilmarnock bonnet. According to Stewart of Garth, the regiment adopted a red hackle in about 1777.

1/73rd (Lord McLeod's) Highlanders

Raised in 1777 (840 Highlanders, 236 Lowland Scots and 34 English and Irish). Initially it served in the garrison of Jersey but was sent to Madras in 1779, where it served against Haider Ali and his son Tippoo Sahib. Fought at Conjeveram (Flank companies only), Porto Novo, Sholungar, Arnee and Cuddalore. Became 71st Highlanders in 1786.

2/73rd Highlanders

Raised in 1778 and sent to Gibraltar, remaining there throughout the siege. Disbanded in 1783 and those officers senior to their 1st Battalion counterparts were allowed to go out to India to join that Battalion, displacing the junior men.

Uniform(both battalions): Buff facings. Thin silver braid for officers and white lace with a single red line on the outside set in square-end loops for the ORs. Tartan was the government sett with one red and two buff overstripes. White pantaloons were worn in India and an inspection report on the 2nd Battalion at Gibraltar after the siege mentions tartan jackets made from old plaids, with white linen trousers.

74th (Campbell's) Highlanders

Raised in 1778, half in Argyllshire and half in Glasgow and the Lowlands. Sent to Halifax later that year. The Flank companies served in the south, most notably at the siege of Charleston while the Battalion companies took part in the seizure of Penobscot (Maine) and thereafter formed its garrison. Disbanded in 1783.

Uniform: Bright yellow facings. Thin silver braid for officers set in pairs; ORs had white square-end loops with single red line. Tartan was the undifferenced government sett.

76th (MacDonald's) Highlanders

Raised in 1778. Seven companies were comprised of Highlanders, mainly from the Western Isles, two of Lowland Scots, and one was Irish. Sent to New York in the summer of 1779. The Flank companies were then detached; the Light company went to 2nd Light Infantry. The Grenadiers remained in New York but the rest of the regiment then served in the south at Petersburg, Green Spring and Yorktown. Disbanded 1784.

Uniform: Deep green facings. Probably gold braid for officers; ORs had white square-end loops with a dark blue line, probably arranged in pairs. Tartan is unrecorded but was most likely the undifferenced government sett.

77th (Murray's) Highlanders

Raised in Perthsire in 1778. Served in Ireland until 1783, then sent to Portsmouth with the intention that they should go to India. However, they mutinied and refused to embark, and were consequently disbanded.

Uniform: Red facings (1778), perhaps green later? Silver braid for officers. Tartan was the government sett with a red overstripe.

78th (Seaforth's) Highlanders

Raised in Ross-shire in 1778, but also including some 200 Lowland Scots. Intended for service in India but temporarily reinforced garrison of Jersey and took part in defence of that island against the French. Finally embarked for India in 1781 but were attacked by a 'putrid fever' and scurvy, resulting in a long stop-over at St Helena and the loss of some 230 men on the voyage. Fought at Cuddalore and Palacatcherry. Became 72nd Highlanders in 1786.

Uniform: Yellow facings, although a 1778 inspection report describes them as orange. Silver braid for officers, worn in bastion loops according to a watercolour by David Alien. ORs white bastion loops with bluish green line. Tartan was the undifferenced government sett.

Next page, The Thin Red Line, painted by Robert Gibb, depicting the 93rd Highlanders stopping an attack by Russian cavalry at the battle of Balaklava in 1854.

81st (Gordon's) Highlanders

Raised in Aberdeenshire in 1778 by William Gordon of Fyvie. Served in Ireland until 1783, then sent to Portsmouth with the intention of being shipped to India but after the 77th mutinied they too were disbanded.

Uniform: White facings. Silver epaulettes and buttons for officers, but no braid. Two portraits survive, one noted by C.C.P. Lawson and another in the Scottish United Services Museum. Tartan was the undifferenced government sett.

1/84th Royal Highland Emigrants

Raised in Canada in 1775, initially from former members of the 42nd, 77th and 78th Highlanders who had been discharged there at the end of the Seven Years' War. Remained in Canada throughout the war, serving most notably in the defence of Quebec in 1775/76. Disbanded in 1784.

2/84th Royal Highland Emigrants

Embodied in Nova Scotia in 1775, partly composed as above but with a substantial number of men recruited i n North Carolina. Five companies remained in Nova Scotia throughout the war but the others, including the Flank companies, served in the south and fought at Eutaw Springs. Disbanded 1784.

Uniform (both Battalions): Blue facings. Gold braid or embroidery for officers. ORs white lace with a blue line between two red ones in square-end loops arranged in pairs. Tartan was the government sett with red overstripe. A flat blue bonnet is shown in a Von Germann watercolour but officers' portraits show Kilmarnock bonnets and in at least one case a gilt thistle badge worn on the cockade (Major John Small).

THE REVOLUTIONARY AND NAPOLEONIC WARS

All regiments wore open, lapelled jackets with white waistcoats until 1797, then single breasted jackets thereafter. Unless otherwise noted, headgear normally comprised dark blue knitted Kilmarnock bonnets with a diced band, a black cockade on left side, a white over red hackle, and black ostrich feathers. It appears to have been common to lose these feathers on active service and wear hummel or bare Kilmarnock bonnets.

1/42nd Royal Highland Regiment

In Scotland at the outbreak of the Revolutionary Wars and served in Low Countries 1793-1795, most notably at Geldermalsen. Brought up to strength by drafts from 97th, 116th, 132nd and 133rd Highlanders and then sent to West Indies with Sir Ralph Abercrombie's expedition 1796-1797. Absorbed 79th Highlanders' effectives before returning and posted almost immediately to Gibraltar. Served Minorca 1798, Egypt 1801, the Peninsula 1808-1809 and Walcheren. Returned to Peninsula 1812-1814, and at Quatre Bras/ Waterloo in 1815.

2/42nd Royal Highland Regiment

Raised in 1803. Served in Peninsula 1810-1812. Effectives then drafted into 1st Battalion. Disbanded in 1814.

Uniform (both battalions): Dark blue facings, Jews Harp bastion loops with red line on outside for rank and file, white silk lace for sergeants and gold lace for officers. Kilt was government or "Black Watch" sett with single red overstripe for all companies (not restricted to grenadiers) until about 1812, and then the undifferenced sett thereafter. All-red hackle worn in bonnet after Geldermalsen in 1795. Plain blue Kilmarnock bonnet worn in undress. Brownish white goatskin purse or sporran worn in full dress.

1/71st Highlanders

Raised in 1777 as 2/73rd but re-numbered in 1786. In Madras at outbreak of war. Flank companies served at Pondicherry and Ceylon until 1797. Posted to Ireland 1800-1805, then to Cape of Good Hope 1806, before being captured during disastrous Buenos Aires expedition. Served in Peninsula 1808-1809 and at Walcheren. Trained as Light Infantry before returning to Peninsula 1810-1814, and served at Quatre Bras/Waterloo in 1815.

2/71st Highlanders

Raised in 1803, but saw no foreign service before being disbanded in 1814.

Uniform: Buff facings, square-ended loops with red line on outside. Officers were unlaced with silver appointments. Tartan was government set with buff and red overstripes until c1798, then white and red overstripes – two vertical red overstripes appeared on kilt apron. White trousers were worn in India. Kilts were worn at Cape and in South America, then tartan pantaloons 1808-c1809. Officially "de-kilted" 1809 and thereafter largely in grey trousers, although some kilts noted in later inspection reports. Round hats were worn in India, then feathered Kilmarnock bonnets until 1809. Thereafter the Kilmarnock bonnets were stripped of feathers and blocked up into the shape of the military cap – officers, however, wore ordinary caps. An odd painting of the regiment on the march shows these blocked bonnets worn with kilts. Brownish purse worn in full dress.

1/72nd Highlanders

Raised in 1778 as 78th, but re-numbered in 1786. In Madras at outbreak of war and remained there until 1797. Served in Ireland 1800-1805 and then at Cape of Good Hope 1806-1821.

2/72nd Highlanders

Raised 1803. Served in Ireland until disbanded 1814.

Uniform: Yellow facings, "Jews Harp" bastion loops with green line on outside, silver lace for officers. Undifferenced government sett. "De-kilted" 1809. Flat blue bonnets worn in undress. White purse.

1/73rd Highlanders

Raised in 1780 as 2/42nd (Royal Highland Regt.) but re-numbered in 1786. In Madras at outbreak of war and remained there until 1805. Briefly home and then served New South Wales 1809-1816.

2/73rd Highlanders

Raised 1809. Served in north Germany and Holland 1813-1814, and at Quatre Bras/Waterloo in 1815. Disbanded in 1816.

Uniform: Dark green facings, "Jews Harp" bastion loops on inside. Broad gold lace for officers arranged in Footguards' style, ie; edging the facings rather than in loops (the Footguards were unimpressed and complained). Government sett with red overstripe (inherited from 42nd), and brown purse. "De-kilted" in 1809.

74th (Argyll) Highlanders

Raised in 1787 by Sir Archibald Campbell specifically for service in India and remained there until 1805. Served at Seringapatam 1792, Flank companies at Pondicherry 1793, then Seringapatam again 1799, Assaye and Argaum. Returned home to serve at Walcheren in 1809 and in the Peninsula 1811-1814.

Uniform: White facings, square-ended loops with red line on outside. Gold lace for officers. White trousers and round hats were worn in India and then "de-kilted" in 1809. May have worn government sett with single white overstripe from 1805-1809 – their tartan was ordered to be distinguished by one when permitted by Adjutant General to resume Highland dress in 1846.

75th (Stirlingshire) Highlanders

Raised 1787 by Colonel Robert Abercromby specifically for service in India and served in Madras until 1805. Recruiting was slow after its return and regiment did not go abroad again until 1811 when sent to Sicily, and then on to Corfu in 1814.

Uniform: Yellow facings, square-ended loops arranged in pairs, with two yellow and one red line. Silver lace for officers. White trousers and round hats were worn in India. Tartan worn on return was probably the undifferenced government sett – there is no evidence for the yellow overstripe mentioned in some secondary sources. "De-kilted" 1809. Officers still wore a large thistle badge on front of their military caps.

1/78th (Ross-shire Buffs)

Letters of service granted to Francis Humberstone Mackenzie (afterwards Lord Seaforth) on 8 March 1793. Served in Low Countries 1794-1795, Cape of Good Hope 1796, and India 1797-1811 – Ahmednugger, Assaye and Argaum, then Java 1811-1816.

2/78th (a)

Raised in February 1794. Served at Cape of Good Hope, then drafted into 1/78th June 1796.

2/78th (b)

Raised in 1804. Initially trained as Light Infantry at Shorncliffe before being posted to Gibraltar in 1805 and Sicily in 1806. Served at Maida. Sent to Egypt in 1807. A draft intended for 1/78th was diverted to Walcheren before eventually going out to India in 1810. Rest of Battalion served in Holland and Belgium 1813-1816. Officers placed on half pay in that year and effectives drafted into 1/78th on its return from India in 1817.

Uniform: Very pale buff facings – virtually off-white. "Flower-pot" bastion loops with green line on outside. Officers initially with gold lace, but later unlaced

with gilt appointments. Tartan was government sett with white and red overstripes – a single vertical red overstripe appearing in centre of kilt apron as a distinction from the two red stripes appearing on the front of 71st kilts – both regiments otherwise had same tartan. White purse. Blue Kilmarnock bonnet with pale buff b and worn in undress.

1/79th (Cameron) Highlanders

Letters of Service granted to Allan Cameron of Erracht 17 August 1793. Served in Low Countries 1794-1795. Went to West Indies with Sir Ralph Abercrombie's expedition and served on Martinique 1795-1797. Effectives drafted into 42nd and regiment recruited afresh. Served on Guernsey 1798, on Helder Expedition 1799, Ferrol 1800 and Egypt 1801, Copenhagen 1807, the Peninsula 1808-1809. At Walcheren and then returned to Peninsula 1810-1814. Served at Quatre Bras/Waterloo 1815

2/79th

Raised in 1804, but saw no foreign service before being disbanded in 1814.

Uniform: Green facings, square-end loops in pairs with two red lines and a central yellow line in lace. Gold lace for officers. Tartan was Cameron of Erracht sett – a fairly complex green sett with numerous red and a few yellow overstripes. White over black purse. White trousers worn in West Indies and blue ones mentioned in 1798 inspection report. Grey trousers worn during last year of Peninsular War.

1/91st (Argyllshire) Highlanders

Letters of Service as 98th Duncan Campbell of Lochnell 10 February 1794, but re-numbered in 1798. Served at Cape of Good Hope 1795-1803, then the Hannover expedition 1805. Went to Peninsula 1808-1809, the Walcheren expedition and then back to Peninsula 1812-1814. Served in Belgium and

Next page, Quatre Bras: Black Watch at Bay, **painted by B. Wollen, depicting the battle of Quatre Bras, part of the Waterloo campaign 1815.**

France 1815. Although officially "de-kilted" in 1809, the regiment successfully maintained its Highland identity.

2/91st

Raised in 1803. Served in Germany and Holland 1814 – including Bergen-op-Zoom. Disbanded later in 1814.

Uniform: Yellow facings, square end loops in pairs with black dart on outside and black line inside. Officers unlaced with silver appointments. Tartan was probably undifferenced government sett prior to "de-kilting" in 1809. Flat blue bonnets worn in undress.

1/92nd (Gordon) Highlanders

Letters of Service as 100th granted to George Gordon, Marquis of Huntly 10 February 1794, but re-numbered in 1798. Served Gibraltar and Corsica 1795-1797, Ireland 1798, Helder Expedition 1799, Egypt 1801 and Copenhagen 1807. Served in Peninsula 1808-1809, at Walcheren and again in Peninsula 1810-1814 – most notably at Maya (see main text). Fought at Quatre Bras/Waterloo in 1815.

2/92nd

Raised in 1803, served in Ireland until disbanded in 1814.

Uniform: Light yellow facings, square-end loops in pairs with blue line on outside. Silver lace with black line for officers. Government sett tartan with single yellow overstripe, white purse in full dress. Flat blue bonnet worn in undress. White trousers were worn in Mediterranean 1795-1797 and Highland dress only resumed in Ireland. Wore grey trousers during last year of Peninsular War.

1/93rd (Sutherland) Highlanders

Letters of Service granted to William Wemys of Wemyss in May 1800 and largely raised from former personnel of disbanded Sutherland Fencibles (q.v.). Served at Cape of Good Hope 1806-1814, then America – New Orleans in 1815.

2/93rd

Raised 1813, served Newfoundland 1814-1815. Disbanded 1815.

Uniform: Yellow facings, pointed "Coldstream" loops in pairs with yellow line on outside. Silver lace for officers. Undifferenced government sett and black purse. 1st Battalion wore tartan trousers and hummel bonnets at New Orleans. Bonnets had "Sutherland" dicing – a plain red/white checquer.

97th (Inverness-shire) Highlanders:

Letters of Service granted to Sir James Grant of Grant on 8th February 1794. Initially served in Guernsey, but then put aboard the Channel Fleet to serve as Marines. Drafted in August 1795 with both Flank companies going to the 42nd and the Battalion companies into the Marines.

Uniform: Green facings, square-end loops in pairs, probably with red and green lines. Gold lace for officers. Government sett with single red overstripe; tartan trousers normally worn instead of kilts. Plain blue Kilmarnock bonnets without feathers worn in most orders of dress. White trousers and round hats worn while serving with Channel Fleet.

109th (Aberdeenshire) Highlanders

Letters of Service granted to Alexander Leith-Hay on 2 April 1794. Served in Channel Islands and assigned to Abercrombie's expedition to the West Indies, but instead drafted into 53rd Foot in August 1795.

Uniform: Light yellow facings, square-end loops. Lace pattern unknown. Silver lace for officers. Feathered Kilmarnock bonnets with green hackles worn by officers, but otherwise all ranks appear to have worn round hats and white trousers, not Highland dress.

116th (Perthshire) Highlanders

Letters of Service granted to Earl of Breadalbane on 10 April 1794. Served in Ireland until drafted into 42nd in August 1795.

Uniform: White or very pale yellow facings, square-end loops in pairs. Lace pattern unknown. Officers had silver lace with black border. Kilt was government sett with double yellow overstripe; black purse.

132nd Highlanders

Letters of Service granted to Duncan Cameron on 11 September 1794 but probably never completed before being drafted into 42nd in August 1795.

Uniform: unknown – probably black facings.

133rd (Inverness Volunteers)

Letters of Service granted to Simon Fraser 22 August 1794 but probably never completed before being drafted into 42nd in August 1795.

Uniform: unknown – probably black facings.

Royal Glasgow Regiment (Un-numbered unit)

Letters of Service granted to Colonel Hugh Montgomerie on 28 August 1794. Not officially a Highland unit, but officers may have worn Highland dress before the regiment was drafted into 37th, 44th and 55th Foot in August 1795 – see West Lowland Fencibles (q.v.).

Uniform: Green facings. Silver lace for officers with loops arranged in pairs. Officers almost certainly had feathered Kilmarnock bonnets and may well have worn kilts of undifferenced government sett. Rank and file probably in round hats and white trousers.

HIGHLAND FENCIBLE REGIMENTS

Fencible regiments were initially raised in Scotland for home service only, although the terms of service were progressively widened to allow for service in England, in Ireland and ultimately anywhere in Europe.

Argyll Fencibles

Letters of Service granted to Duke of Argyll in July 1759. Served in Scotland until disbanded in 1763.

Uniform: Red single-breasted jacket and waistcoat, undifferenced government sett.

Sutherland Fencibles

Letters of Service granted to Earl of Sutherland in July 1759. According to Stewart of Garth, upwards of 260 men in the regiment were above 5' 11" in height and so both Flank companies were designated as Grenadiers. Served in Scotland until disbanded in 1763.

Uniform: Red single breasted jacket and waistcoat (including field officers according to portrait of Earl), yellow facings and thin silver lace for officers. Undifferenced government sett.

Argyll (or Western) Fencibles

Raised by Lord Frederick Campbell and embodied at Glasgow in April 1778. Mainly recruited in Argyllshire but included substantial contingent from Glasgow and south-west Scotland. Normally commanded by Major Hugh Montgomerie of Coilsfield. Served in Scotland until disbanded in 1783.

Uniform: Yellow facings, silver lace for officers – possibly bastion loops. Undifferenced government sett.

Northern Fencibles

Raised by Duke of Gordon and embodied at Aberdeen in 1778. Served in Scotland until disbanded in 1783.

Uniform: Yellow facings, silver lace for oficers. Undifferenced government sett. Kilmarnock bonnets adorned with yellow worsted "feathers" in place of black ostrich from May 1780.

Sutherland Fencibles

Letters of Service granted to William Wemyss of Wemyss (nephew of late Earl) and embodied at Fort George in February 1779. Served in Edinburgh area until disbanded in 1783.

Uniform: Yellow facings, silver lace for officers. Undifferenced government sett.

Aberdeen (Princess of Wales) Fencibles

Raised by Colonel Leith in 1794. Served in Ireland until disbanded on 11 April 1802.

Uniform: Lemon yellow facings, square-end loops. Silver lace for officers. Kilt: undifferenced government sett, white purse.

Angus Fencibles

Raised in 1794 and disbanded in 1802.

Uniform: Yellow facings. Kilt: undifferenced government sett, white purse. Tartan trousers also recorded.

Argyll (or Western) Fencibles

Raised in 1793 by Marquis of Lorne for service in Scotland only. Disbanded in 1799.

Uniform: Pale yellow facings, square-end loops, silver lace for officers. Kilt: undifferenced government sett, white purse.

1st Argyll Fencibles

Raised in 1794 by Colonel Henry Clavering. Served in Ireland before being disbanded in 1802.

Uniform: Medium blue facings and fringe on shoulder straps. Kilt: undifferenced Government sett, white purse.

2nd Argyll Fencibles

Letters of Service granted to Colonel Archibald McNeil of Colonsay on 17 July 1798 for service in Europe. Subsequently served in Gibraltar garrison until disbanded on 3 July 1802.

Uniform: Yellow facings and fringe on shoulder straps. Kilt: undifferenced government sett, white purse.

Banffshire (Duke of York's) Fencibles

Letters of service granted to Colonel Hay 26 July 1798 for service in Europe. Disbanded 10 May 1802.

Uniform: Blue facings. Kilt: undifferenced government sett, white purse.

1/Breadalbane & 2/Breadalbane Fencibles

Raised by Earl of Breadalbane in 1793 for service in Scotland only. Disbanded in 1799.

Uniform: Hamilton Smith shows yellow facings but surviving coat has white or very pale yellow/buff facings. Silver lace with black border for officers. Kilt: government sett with double yellow overstripe., black purse.

3/Breadalbane Fencibles (Glenorchy Battalion)

Raised in 1794 and served in Ireland until disbanded on 28 July 1802.

Uniform: probably as above although Hamilton Smith shows a red overstripe on the tartan.

Next page, Alma: Forward the 42nd, **painted by Robert Gibb, depicting the Black Watch at the battle of the Alma during the Crimean War in 1854.**

Caithness Legion

Raised in 1794 by Sir Benjamin Dunbar of Hempriggs and served in Ireland.

Uniform: Yellow facings, silver lace for officers. Tartan trousers worn – probably undifferenced government sett; white purse.

Dumbarton Fencibles

Letters of Service granted to Campbell of Stonefield on 11 October 1794 for service anywhere in the British Isles. Served on Guernsey in 1795 and then Ireland in 1797. Disbanded 5 October 1802.

Uniform: Black facings. Kilt of undifferenced government sett – tartan trousers also recorded. Hose had black/grey check on white instead of usual red/pink on white.

Elgin Fencibles

Raised in 1794 by Earl of Elgin for service anywhere in the British Isles and disbanded on 15 October 1803.

Uniform: Green facings. Kilt: undifferenced government sett, with white purse. Tartan trousers also recorded.

Fraser Fencibles

Raised by Colonel Simon Fraser in 1794 for service anywhere in the British Isles and embodied at Inverness on 14 June 1795. Served in Ireland 1798 and disbanded at Glasgow in July 1802.

Uniform: Black facings. Kilt: apparently Fraser tartan – basically a red sett. Non-contemporary illustration of Battle of Castlebar shows tartan trousers.

Glengarry Fencibles

Raised in 1794 by Alexander McDonnell of Glengarry for service anywhere in British Isles. Served on Jersey and Guernsey.

Uniform: Yellow facings. Kilt: probably undifferenced government sett, with white purse although it is possible that Glengarry sett may have been worn – perhaps only by officers. Sutherland dicing on bonnet.

Gordon (Northern) Fencibles

Letters of Service granted to Duke of Gordon on 3 March 1793 for service in Scotland, although later extended to England. Disbanded in 1798.

Uniform: Lemon yellow facings, square-end loops in pairs. Silver lace for officers. Kilt: Government sett with single yellow overstripe, white purse. Black leather equipment.

Loyal Inverness Fencibles

Letters of Service granted to Major Baillie of Dunean on 21 November 1794 for service anywhere in British Isles, but not embodied at Inverness unril October 1795. Served in Ireland in 1798 and re-titled "Duke of York's Royal Inverness-shire Highlanders". Disbanded at Stirling in March 1802.

Uniform: Originally yellow facings, but these were changed to blue in 1798. Silver lace for officers. Kilt said to be of Baillie tartan – basically a light or medium blue sett.

Regiment of the Isles

Letters of Service granted to Lord MacDonald in 1799 and embodied at Inverness on 4 June in that year. Served in England until disbanded at Fort George in July 1802.

Uniform: Yellow facings. Gold lace for officers. Kilt may have been a MacDonald sett.

Lochaber Fencibles

Letters of Service granted to Donald Cameron of Locheil on 17 July 1798 for service in Europe, but actually served in Ireland until disbanded on 26 June 1802.

Uniform: Black facings. Kilt: undifferenced government sett, white purse. All white hackle in bonnet.

Princess Charlotte of Wales' Fencibles

Letters of Service granted to Colonel John Macleod of Colbecks on 19 July 1798 for service in Europe, but actually served in Ireland until disbanded at Taymouth Barracks on 11 June 1802.

Uniform: Yellow facings. Kilt: undifferenced government sett. All-white hackle in bonnet.

Perthshire Fencibles

Letters of Service granted to Colonel William Roberston of Lude in 1794 but never completed.

Uniform: Yellow facings. Kilt: undifferenced government sett, white purse.

Reay Fencibles

Raised by Colonel Mackay Hugh Baillie of Rosehall in 1794 for service anywhere in British Isles. Embodied at Fort George in March 1795 and therafter served in Ireland – most notably at Tara Hill.

Uniform: Greyish blue facings, square-end loops set in pairs. Silver lace for officers. Kilt: Mackay tartan – basically a green sett. Badger purses for officers and sergeants, white goatskin for rank and file. Officers normally wore fur-crested round hats and white pantaloons.

Ross-shire Fencibles

Two company unit raised by Major Colin Mackenzie of Mountgerald in 1796.

Uniform: Yellow facings. Kilt: Government sett with single red overstripe.

Ross and Cromarty Rangers

Letters of Service granted to Colonel Lewis Mackenzie, younger of Scatwell, on 8 August 1798 for service anywhere in Europe – but actually stationed in Aberdeen. Disbanded on 27 July 1802.

Uniform: Yellow facings. Kilt: Government sett with single red overstripe.

1/Rothesay and Caithness Fencibles

Raised by Sir John Sinclair of Ulbster for service in Scotland only and embodied at Inverness in October 1794. Disbanded in 1799.

Uniform: Yellow facings, square-end loops with blue line in lace. Silver lace for officers. Tartan trousers – government sett with single yellow overstripe, white purse. Red, yellow and white hackle in bonnet.

2/Rothesay and Caithness Fencibles

Raised in 1795 by Sir John Sinclair for service anywhere in British Isles and embodied at Forfar in May of that year. Served in Ireland before being disbanded on 26 July 1802.

Uniform: as for 1st Battalion, although red waistcoats may have been worn by way of distinction.

Royal Clan Alpine Fencibles

Letters of Service granted to Colonel Alexander Macgregor Murray 31 July 1798 for service anywhere in Europe. Embodied at Stirling in May 1799 and served in Ireland until disbanded on 24 July 1802.

Uniform: Blue facings and fringe on shoulder-straps. Kilt: undifferenced government sett.

Strathspey (Grant) Fencibles

Raised by Sir James Grant of Grant for service in Scotland only. Embodied at Forres April in April 1793 and disbanded in 1799, having twice mutinied in the meantime.

Uniform: Green facings, square-end loops in pairs. Gold lace for officers. Kilt: Government sett with single red overstripe. Badger purses for officers, white goatskin for NCOs and men. Light company wore plain blue Kilmarnock bonnets. Officers usually wore fur-crested round hats and white breeches.

Sutherland Fencibles

Raised by Colonel William Wemyss of Wemyss in 1793 for service in Scotland only, but volunteered in 1797 for service in Ireland, before being disbanded in 1799.

Uniform: Yellow facings, "flower pot" bastion loops. Silver lace for officers. Kilt: undifferenced government sett, black purse. Sutherland dicing on bonnet.

West Lowland Fencibles

Raised in Glasgow and south-west Scotland in 1793 by Colonel Hugh Montgomerie of Coilsfield for service in Scotland only. Wore Highland uniform.

Uniform: Green facings, square-ended loops in pairs. Silver lace for officers. Rank and file in tartan trousers – undifferenced government sett – officers, however, wore kilts and belted plaids. All ranks wore feathered Kilmarnock bonnets. Similar uniform probably worn by Montgomerie's short-lived regular Royal Glasgow Regiment.

Next page, the Scottish Regiments of the British Army in 1895, painted by R. Simkin for *The Boy's Own* paper. *Front rank, left to right:* Seaforth Highlanders, corporal and piper; Royal Scots, Queen's Own Cameron Highlanders, private and sergeant; The Cameronians, officer; Black Watch, officer; Highland Light Infantry, officer, Princess Louise's Argyll and Sutherland Highlanders, officer; Royal Scots Fusiliers, officer; Princess Louise's Argyll and Sutherland Highlanders, piper; Scots Guards, private; Gordon Highlanders, private; The King's Own Scottish Borderers, colour-sergeant; Black Watch, drummer. *Rear rank, left to right:* 2nd Dragoons, Royal Scots Greys, trooper; Queen's Own Cameron Highlanders, field-officer, Gordon Highlanders, field-officer, 2nd Dragoons, Royal Scots Greys, officer.

BIBLIOGRAPHY

Anton, James, *Retrospect of a Military Life during the most eventful periods of the last war.* Edinburgh, 1841.

Bland, Humphrey, *A Treatise of Military Discipline,* 1727.

Brown, Iain Gordon & Cheape, Hugh, *Witness to Rebellion; John Maclean's Journal of the 'Forty-Five, and the Penicuik Drawings,* Tuckwell Press, 1996. A truly astonishing set of contemporary sketches depicting Jacobite and regular soldiers. Of particular interest are the number of clansmen depicted with firelock and bayonet.

Bulloch, J.M., *Territorial Soldiering in North-East Scotland,* New Spalding Club, Aberdeen, 1914.

Bumstead, J.M., *The People's Clearance; Highland Emigration to British North America 1770-1815,* Edinburgh University, 1982. A very useful corrective to the 'Highlanders as victims' school.

Grant, George, *New Highland Military Discipline,* London, 1757.

Houlding, John, *Fit for Service: The Training of the British Army 1715-1795,* Clarendon Press, 1981.

Lenman, Bruce, *The Jacobite Clans of the Great Glen,* Methuen, 1984.

Mackay, W., *Urquhart and Glenmoriston,* Inverness, 1914.

Maclean, Loraine, *Indomitable Colonel; biography of Sir Alan Cameron of Erracht,* Shepheard-Walwyn, 1986.

Prebble, John, *Mutiny; Highland Regiments in Revolt, 1743-1804,* Secker & Warburg, 1975. Vivid and detailed accounts of a number of incidents, but marred by taking them out of context.

Reid, Stuart, *The Campaigns of Montrose,* Mercat Press, 1990.

Reid, Stuart, *Like Hungry Wolves; Culloden Moor 16 April 1746,* Windrow & Greene 1994.

Reid, Stuart, *1745; A Military History of the Last Jacobite Rising,* Spellmount, 1996.

Reid, Stuart, *Wellington's Highlanders,* Osprey, 1992.

Reid, Stuart, *18th Century Highlanders,* Osprey, 1993.

Reid, Stuart, *Highland Clansman 1689-1746,* Osprey, 1997.

Scobie, I.H. Mackay, *An Old Highland Fencible Corps; The History of the Reay Fencible Highland Regiment of Foot, or Mackay's Highlanders 1794-1802,* Blackwood & Sons, 1914.

Stevenson, David, *Alasdair MacCholla and the Highland Problem of the 17th Century,* John Donald, Edinburgh, 1980.

Stewart, Col. David, of Garth, *Sketches of the Character,Manners and Present State of the Highlanders of Scotland; with details of the Military Service of the Highland Regiment,* 2nd Edition, Edinburgh, 1822. Stewart served in the 1/42nd and 2/78th Highlanders during the Revolutionary and Napoleonic Wars. His two-volume *Sketches* are a mixture of oral and documentary testimony as to the services of the various Highland regiments from the raising of the Black Watch to Waterloo. In places his statements need to be treated with some caution, and he firmly promoted the belief that Highlanders were 'stormers', but on the whole his book is absolutely invaluable.

Wallace, John, *Scottish Swords and Dirks,* Arms and Armour, 1970.

HIGHLANDER DIRECTORY

Re-enactment Groups

Clansmen

The Atholl Highlanders (Lace Wars).
Contact: Tony Carter, Miltown of
Craigellie, Fraserburgh, Aberdeenshire
AB43 8SP, email: junetc@aol.com; or
contact: Andy Burbidge, Flat 74, Wingate
Court, Aldershot, Hampshire, England,
email: andrew.robertson@nokia.com

Bagot's Hussars (Independent).
Contact: Jeffrey Burn, Old Buittle Tower,
Dalbeattie, Kirkcudbrightshire SG7 1PA.

Clan Donnachaidh
(Inchbrackie's Regiment 1644-1646/
The Atholl Brigade 1745-1746).
Contact: Brian T. Carpenter,
422 State Route 7, Port Crane NY 13833,
USA, email: bcarp@gateway.net

Fraser's Highlanders (Lace Wars).
Contact: Bill Kane, 8 Millburn Road,
Westfield, Bathgate, West Lothian,
EH48 3BT, email:
trotsky@kremlin.swinternet.co.uk;
or contact:
Stuart Orme, 302 Princes Road, Penkull,
Stoke on Trent, Staffordshire, ST4 7JP,
email: Frasers@annongul.Screaming.Net

Wallace Clan Trust.
Contact: Seoras Wallace, Clan Studios,
Carig House, 68 Darnley Street,
Pollockshields, Glasgow G41 2SE.

Regulars

The Watch: 43rd/42nd Highlanders
(Lace Wars). Contact: Keith Jepson,
52 Balcombe Road, Horley,
Surrey RH6 9AA.

42nd Royal Highland Regiment (1815).
Contact: Glenn Robinson, 39 St.Davids
Road, All Hallows by the Sea, Rochester,
Kent ME3 9PW.

79th (Cameron) Highlanders.
Contact: Tom Greenshields,
6 Apollo House, 103 Gilders Road,
Chessington, Surrey KT9 2AY.

93rd Sutherland Highland Regiment
Living History Unit. Contact:
PO Box 100011, Fort Worth TX 76185,
USA, email:ninety3rd@aol.com

Royal Ecossois (Lace Wars).
Contact: c/o 1 Golden Noble Hill,
Colchester, Essex.

Museums

Black Watch* Museum. Balhousie Castle,
Perth, Perthshire, tel: 01738 21281.
*42nd & 73rd Highlanders

The Regimental Museum of
The Highlanders
(Gordon Highlanders Collection).*
St.Luke's, Viewfield Road, Aberdeen
AB15 7XH, tel: 01224 311200.
* 75th & 92nd Highlanders

The Regimental Museum of
The Highlanders (Queen's Own
Highlanders Collection).*
Fort George, Ardersier; correspondence
to c/o RHQ The Highlanders, Cameron
Barracks, Inverness IV2 3XD, tel: 01463
224 380.
*72nd, 78th & 79th Highlanders

Royal Highland Fusiliers* Museum.
518 Sauchiehall Street, Glasgow G2 3LW,
tel: 0141 332 0961.
* includes 71st and 74th Highlanders

Scottish United Services Museum.
The Castle, Edinburgh, EH1 2NG,
tel: 0131 225 7534.

Stirling Regimental Museum*.
Stirling Castle, Stirling FK8 1EJ,
tel: 01786 75165.

*91st & 93rd Highlanders
West Highland Museum. Cameron
Square, Fort William, Inverness-shire,
tel: 01397 702 169.

Historic Sites

Culloden Moor, just five miles outside
Inverness, is well signposted from the
town, and from the A9 (from Perth) and
A92 (from Aberdeen). About one quarter
of the battlefield is in the ownership of
the National Trust for Scotland and
some of the enclosure walls have recently
been reconstructed, although regimental
markers are wrongly placed.

A short distance away is Fort George,
Ardersier, an impressive artillery
fortification and barrack complex which
has served as a home for most Highland
regiments raised since the 1750s.
Still in use as a military barracks, the
fortifications are in the care of Historic
Scotland. It also houses the Regimental
Museum of The Highlanders (Queens
Own Highlanders Colection) and the
Seafield Collection, arms and equipment
formerly used by the 97th Highlanders
and Inverness-shire Militia in the 1790s
and Napoleonic period.

Further down the A9 are the impressive
remains of Ruthven Barracks, the
scene of two brief sieges during the
'45, and the nearby Highland Folk
Museum in Kingussie is also worth
visiting if time allows.

Unfortunately, the A9 crosses the
battlefield of Killiecrankie, running
directly along the position actually
occupied by General Mackay's army.
The Highland army charged down the
steep slope immediately to the north
of the road. The National Trust for
Scotland has a small visitor centre in
the Pass of Killiecrankie.

INDEX

Pianna

*For katie, wishing you the
long pleasure of books*

Mary Lyn Ray

1 March 1995

BY *Mary Lyn Ray*

ILLUSTRATED BY *Bobbie Henba*

Harcourt Brace & Company

San Diego   New York   London

Requests for permission to make copies of any part of the work should be
mailed to: Permissions Department, Harcourt Brace & Company, 8th Floor,
Orlando, Florida 32887.

Library of Congress Cataloging-in-Publication Data
Ray, Mary Lyn.
Pianna/written by Mary Lyn Ray; illustrated by Bobbie Henba.
p.   cm.
Summary: Anna learns to play the piano and continues to play all her life.
ISBN 0-15-261357-9
[1. Piano — Fiction.] I. Henba, Bobbie, ill. II. Title.
PZ7.R210154Pi   1994
[E] — dc20   91-14609

Printed in Singapore

First edition

A B C D E

The paintings in this book were done in Accent Country Colors and Liquitex
acrylics on Fredrix Ultra Smooth Portrait Canvas.
The display type was set in Phaistos and the text type was set in Perpetua by
Harcourt Brace & Company Photocomposition Center, San Diego, California.
Color separations were made by Bright Arts, Ltd., Singapore.
Printed and bound by Tien Wah Press, Singapore
Production supervision by Warren Wallerstein and Ginger Boyer
Designed by Lydia D'moch

For Camille and Julian, and Vera
— M. L. R.

For John H. and Bella — my dad and mom —
grand folks of Pianna's time
— B. H.

Anna's father built a house between the railroad and Ragged Mountain.

He began when the hills were green and grass was new. As he worked, the leaves on the trees colored and fell. Snow came, then grass again and green song. When he finished, orange lilies were opening. And he painted the house orange to remember.

Anna remembers. She and her brothers and sisters were born there, eighty years ago. Anna lives in the orange house still.

In her yard she has the track where trains used to roll right by the house. Six trains a day were as good as a clock back then.

In her kitchen she has a stone sink where water runs cold from the inside of the mountain.

Above the sink she has a shelf where she collects ceramic cows in place of the real cow she had for years.

In her front room she has a piano.

When Anna was a girl, almost every house had an Estey organ that had to be pumped to get any sound. Her house had an organ, too. But pianos were new. Until the summer she was seven, no one in Danbury had a piano.

That summer, Anna's father took her to the variety show sponsored by the Grange.

Outside, tents were set up for refreshments. But Anna didn't buy popcorn. She didn't buy licorice. She didn't ask for lemonade.

She wanted to listen to the show inside. Anna knew hymns and parlor songs. But she had never heard music like this.

She held the music in her head as she and her father drove home.

Then she went to the organ in the parlor. Pumping with one foot, she stood there and played what she had heard at the show.

"Our Anna must be musical," her mother said. Her father said, "Well, I guess she'd better be getting lessons."

And he bought her the piano, which arrived a week later in a big crate.

The piano came from Boston. Anna would have to go there for lessons.

Schoolbooks came from Boston and barley candy at Christmas and the *Post* her father read on Sundays. But Anna had never imagined going there—until she held the yellow ticket.

A professor who had an advertisement in the *Post* agreed to teach her if she would come once a week, on the train.

Anna rode the train to school in Andover every day, so she knew the trip that far. The mysteries began just beyond.

First there was East Andover. Then Franklin, Boscawen, Penacook, Concord (past the statehouse with the great gold dome), Manchester (past the mills on the Merrimack, the biggest woolen mills in the world). Then Nashua, and into Massachusetts: Lowell, Wilmington, Woburn, Medford, Somerville, Boston.

The professor lived in a brownstone house and gave lessons in an extra room.
Tall windows came down to the floor, which was waxed instead of painted like
the floors at home. There was a marble fireplace that never had a fire in it. And on
the piano, a pair of candlesticks strung with prisms quivered when Anna played.

Back home, Anna practiced.

When her brothers asked her to climb trees or pick blueberries up on Ragged, she would rather practice. When her sisters asked her to play dress-up or play store, she would rather practice. Her brothers and sisters called her Pianna.

Every Saturday Anna rode to Boston for a lesson. Her mother made her a satchel out of flour sacks to carry her music in.

When the train rolled to a stop at a station, she listened to the wheels turning slowly around. They seemed to say "adagio," like the word in her music that meant "slow." As the train picked up speed in the flats, then it was "prestissimoprestissimoprestissimo…"

Most times Anna went by herself, a hundred seven and a half miles down and a hundred seven and a half miles back. But sometimes her mother went with her. Then they did extra things, which they called their ceremonies.

Sometimes they rode the swan boats in the park.

Sometimes they had tea at a tea shop up on Beacon Hill, where a huge
copper kettle hung over the door with steam hissing from the spout like steam
from the stack of a train.

Sometimes they stood outside the window of the Boston Music Company.
Other times they actually went in. If Anna had any birthday money, she could
buy music that wasn't assigned.

Twice a year, in winter and spring, there were recitals. Anna wore her best dress and her best shoes and white stockings. Her mother and her father and her brothers and her sisters came and heard her play, and afterwards they all went and had ice cream.

When word got out in Danbury that Anna was taking lessons, she was invited to play at church.

There was no piano at the church, just an old pump organ. Sitting in front of everyone, Anna discovered that her legs were too short to reach the pedals. So Uncle Luther, who was the minister, left the pulpit and pumped so Anna could play.

Every summer Anna's family gave entertainments in a pine grove near their house. In the afternoon they hung lanterns in the trees, which they lighted after dark. All the neighbors came and everyone had a good time. Usually they spoke pieces or sang or put on a tableau. Anna would have played, but the piano was too heavy to carry outdoors.

The morning after, she went looking in the grass for pennies that had fallen out of pockets. She kept them in a jar and used them to buy music.

Anna loved music more than anything until she was seventeen.
Then Clarence, up in town, began to court her, and eventually
persuaded her to be his bride.

Anna's brothers and sisters
had married and moved away,
so Clarence came to live in the house between the railroad and Ragged Mountain.
Now Anna wanted to stay home. She stopped going down to Boston.
But she still played the piano every day.

She played with a baby on her lap. She played while it napped. She played while the clothes dried.

She played while the bread rose, while the stove heated, while the cow grazed.

She played while the beans bloomed in the garden,   while th

right leaves fell,   while snow piles grew against the pumpkin-colored house.

On Sundays she played at churches in Wilmot and New London.

On Tuesdays she played for the Grange.

But mostly she played for herself.

Now the babies have grown and gone. Her parents have died.
Clarence has died. Anna lives alone. The cow is gone, the trains
are gone.

"But I have my piano," says Anna.

And she goes to it and plays.

She may be playing now.